NO PLACE ON EARTH

Ellen Glasgow, James Branch Cabell
And Richmond-in-Virginia

AMS PRESS
NEW YORK

DINNER AT THE CABELLS, 1932—(*l. to r.*) Burton Rascoe, Ellen Glasgow, James Branch Cabell, Mrs. James Branch Cabell, Elliott Springs

NO PLACE ON EARTH

Ellen Glasgow, James Branch Cabell
And Richmond-in-Virginia

By Louis D. Rubin, Jr.

AUSTIN · UNIVERSITY OF TEXAS PRESS

Library of Congress Cataloging in Publication Data

Rubin, Louis Decimus, 1923–
  No place on earth.

  Original ed. published as a supplement to the Texas
quarterly, v. 2, no. 3.
  Includes bibliographical references.
  1. Authors, American--Richmond. 2. Glasgow, Ellen
Anderson Gholson, 1874-1945. 3. Cabell, James Branch,
1879-1958. I. The Texas quarterly. Supplement.
II. Title.
[PS267.R5R8 1973]   813'.5'209   74-161773
ISBN 0-404-09040-0

Reprinted by special permission with the University
of Texas Press, Austin, Texas.

From the edition of 1959, Austin
First AMS edition published in 1973
Manufactured in the United States of America

AMS PRESS INC.
NEW YORK, N. Y.   10003

FOR GUY AND VIRGINIA FRIDDELL

Preface

FIRST OF ALL, it is necessary to say what this book is not. It is not, and does not purport to be, an historical or biographical study of Ellen Glasgow and James Branch Cabell. It is not even a thoroughgoing critical account. I have not discussed all the novels and other works of either writer.

Rather, this book is an informal, even personal commentary on the work of two Virginia authors, in terms of the place from which they came. It has been written in part at least out of dissatisfaction—with the kind of criticism Miss Glasgow's and Mr. Cabell's work has received, with the kind of reputations that both these writers seem to have with most readers.

Much has been written about Ellen Glasgow, and rather less about James Branch Cabell. There has been very little perceptive criticism of Miss Glasgow's work as literature, however, though her place in cultural and literary history has been repeatedly defined. Mr. Cabell has received only somewhat better critical handling, but his little niche in cultural and literary history seems to me to be quite misrepresented.

As will appear evident, I feel that Miss Glasgow's work has been praised rather uncritically, and in general for the wrong reasons, while nowadays Mr. Cabell's work has been remarkably underrated. I wanted to redress that balance a little, to my own satisfaction at least.

Then there is the South. I wanted to do what I think has not yet been done: to try to fit their work into the milieu from which both evolved. As one who has lived in the South for most of my life, much of that time in the same city where both of them lived, it has always seemed to me that the South, and Richmond, Virginia, had a great deal to do with the form their work took.

What follows is an attempt to examine some of these matters. I do not propose to discuss all the writings of Ellen Glasgow and James Branch Cabell, though I think I am tolerably familiar with their work. I have tried instead to single out certain novels and memoirs that seemed to have particular relevance to my inquiry. I found as I went along that my study of Miss Glasgow was evolving more or less along chronological lines, with something of a biographical, even psychological approach. Partly for this reason I have purposely not reviewed her work through the latest versions of the novels as finally revised in the Virginia Edition, but have sought to deal with the novels in the editions that were first published. With Mr. Cabell, on the other hand, the chronological approach did not seem fruitful, and therefore I did not use it. Except in the very earliest novels, there did not appear to me to be any important evolution in technique throughout the author's lifetime. He seemed to me to have arrived at just about his full style in *The Cream of the Jest,* and to have sustained it thereafter with almost no faltering.

I might note, too, that James Branch Cabell struck me as having been more fully conscious of exactly what as a novelist he was doing, and why he was doing it, than any other American author I have ever read save possibly Henry James. Indeed, the one other novelist who seems to me to have been quite as articulate as Mr. Cabell about what he was writing, in the sense of being able to discuss it objectively and broadly, is Marcel Proust. (I am entirely aware, of course, of the dubious literary value of that capability, as well as of the considerable difference between Mr. Cabell's habit of composing commentaries on his novels and Proust's much more architectonic use of the same kind of material in the formal pattern of *The Remembrance of Things Past*.) I do not believe that very much has ever been said about Mr. Cabell's novels that he had not somewhere in his work anticipated and commented on. I knew Mr. Cabell very slightly during the last two years of his life, and he told me once that he enjoyed writing his nonfiction much more than his fiction. I can well believe it. Anyone who has read very much of Mr. Cabell's work surely cannot escape the conviction that James Branch Cabell very much enjoyed being James Branch Cabell—and yet it seems to me, too, that he was a genuinely modest person.

The writing of this study was made possible directly by the author's having received a Guggenheim Fellowship to do work in Southern literature, and I should like to express my considerable gratitude to the John Simon Guggenheim Memorial Foundation, and to the Messrs. Henry Allen Moe and James Mathias, for being thus enabled to undertake it. Other and equally grateful thanks go to President John Rutherford Everett, Dean Mary Phlegar Smith, and Miss Mary Vincent Long, all of Hollins College, for their help and cooperation in enabling me to embark on my Fellowship duties; to Miss Dorothy Doerr and the staff of the Fishburn Library of Hollins College; to Vice-President Harry H. Ransom of the University of Texas, for his continuing personal interest in this project; and to the following individuals, among others, for advice and consultation during the writing of this volume: Mr. Robert D. Jacobs, Mr. John Edward Hardy, Mr. Ellington White, Mr. Allen Tate, Mr. Donald Davidson, Mr. John A. Allen, Mrs. James Branch Cabell, and Mr. C. Hugh Holman.

The picture appearing as frontispiece to the book is the property of Mrs. James Branch Cabell, of Richmond, Virginia, and is used through her kind permission. For permission to quote for purposes of criticism from the published writings of Ellen Glasgow and James Branch Cabell, I should like herewith to make proper and grateful acknowledgment to the publishing firms of Doubleday and Company; Harcourt, Brace and Company; The McBride Company; and Farrar, Straus and Cudahy, all of New York City.

Louis D. Rubin, Jr.

Hollins College, Virginia
January 1959

CONTENTS

NO PLACE ON EARTH

Ellen Glasgow, James Branch Cabell
And Richmond-in-Virginia

PART I
Miss Ellen

1. Prologue: Certain Reservations Concerning What Is To Follow

IN THE VERY EARLY YEARS of the present century, there was con-
ceived the idea of a grand compendium of Southern literature, in
which the numerous achievements of the poets, novelists, and belle-
lettrists of the Southern states could be assembled and displayed to
the world en masse, in order thereby to "enrich the national spirit
by the light it throws upon the life of a sincere and distinctive sec-
tion of the republic."[1]

It was not to be a chauvinistic endeavor. As one of the editors-in-
chief, Edwin Anderson Alderman, explained in his introduction,
"the merely sectional idea reaches a climax of folly and hurtfulness
when it exalts complaisancy and self-satisfaction above open-
mindedness and constant analysis." Rather, the multivolumed an-
thology would be designed "simply to lay before men for their study
and reflection the record of life as revealed in literature." That, and
to "make clear that the literary barrenness of the South has been
overstated, and its contributions to American literature under-
valued, both as to quantity and quality."[2]

To this end, a set of handsomely bound volumes began appearing in 1907, containing in alphabetical order selections from the

3

work of representative Southern writers, together with short introductions to each author prepared by assorted scholars and gentlemen. Each volume included the work of from fifteen to twenty-five writers. The editors tended toward inclusion rather than exclusion, as seemed appropriate in a work to be sold by public subscription. The fourth volume, for example, contained generous selections from the writings of such esteemed literati as Will Allen Dromgoole, Reuben Thomas Durrett, Marguerite E. Easter, Mary McNeil Fenollosa, Oscar Penn Fitzgerald, Henry Lynden Flash, Alcée Fortier, Alice French, and Edwin Wiley Fuller, in addition to the work of somewhat better-known authors such as Thomas Dixon, Jr., Harry Stillwell Edwards, William Elliott, John Fox, Jr., Charles Gayarré, Basil L. Gildersleeve, Caroline Gilman—and Ellen Glasgow.

The introductions were for the most part descriptive and laudatory, for the editors sought to secure commentators who were not only acquainted with the work of the authors, but generally sympathetic and well disposed toward it. "While it is obvious that in this method there has been a loss in uniformity and perhaps in soberness and reserve of judgment," declared the literary editor of the work, Charles W. Kent, in his prefatory remarks, "there has been a marked gain in freshness and variety of treatment, in personal and vital estimates, and in individuality."[3]

From Miss Ellen Glasgow's work, the editors chose brief passages from *The Battle-Ground, The Deliverance,* and *The Ancient Law,* together with poems entitled "The Freeman" and "A Creed." To provide a preface, Mr. Rosewell Page of Virginia was approached, and accepted the assignment. A lawyer, Page was brother to the renowned Thomas Nelson Page and a dabbler in verse and prose himself, as well as a classical scholar and a moderately successful politician. Also like his more famous brother, he was a fervent admirer of the Old South, and tended to look with distaste upon that which was crass and sordid in modern literature. Even so, he was a Virginia gentleman, and might be expected to smile indulgently upon a young Richmond lady whose novels, despite certain

4

unfortunate passages, were after all attracting so much attention everywhere, and were, for the work of a young woman, quite remarkable. Indeed, she had already published some seven novels, as well as a book of poems.

So Rosewell Page bent to his task and produced for the *Library of Southern Literature* an introduction to Ellen Glasgow's work that was notable, one might say, for its restraint. Miss Glasgow, he pointed out, came of good Virginia stock. Though to some it might seem odd that a young woman scarce thirty-five years of age could possess knowledge of certain matters, still, was this not true of such writers as Fanny Burney as well? The answer, Mr. Page ventured, was simply genius, "the divine afflatus."[4]

He could not of course quite go along with some of Miss Glasgow's aberrations. "If her work does not appeal to certain people," he felt it necessary to remark, "in spite of the fact that her books have been among the great sellers on their first appearance, it is due to the choice of subjects and the somber covering with which they are clad." As for Rosewell Page himself, he would be broad-minded, and perhaps a trifle noncommittal: "In her choice and treatment of her subjects she is nearer to Ibsen than to George Eliot." Perhaps the most revealing sentence in Mr. Page's encomium is his comment on Miss Glasgow's second novel, *Phases of an Inferior Planet*. That work, he declared, "is in many respects real; *but* the keynote is one of pessimism."[5] [Italics mine]

In the telltale use of that conjunction to join those two clauses there spoke not only Rosewell Page but generations of Southern thought. For the brother of Thomas Nelson Page, that which was really accurate and true to life must perforce be optimistic. The somber, the pessimistic were, if not quite unreal, then at any rate certainly far from the whole truth. One must always look on the pleasant side; to do otherwise was in bad taste. He summed it all up a few years later in a eulogy of Thomas Nelson Page. His brother's goal, Rosewell Page explained, "was to weave about the time and place of which he wrote some love-story or romance which should accurately portray the life of the period. He was not attempting the 'problem novels,' which profess to cure the ills of life by parading them.* He did not believe the province of a novelist to be that of a scavenger, nor that it was the author's duty to be dealing with the physical or moral filth of the sewer or backstairs."[6]

In so saying, Rosewell Page spoke for Virginia. Whatever might have been transpiring politically and socially in the Old Dominion during the decades when Ellen Glasgow was growing up and beginning her early novels, its literature at any rate had not often been soiled by the clay of everyday life. Thomas Nelson Page with his heart-warming tales of noble aristocrats, pristine belles, and faithful darkies; Mary Johnston and her exotic historical romances of colonial Virginia—these were the two most admired of literary Virginians. Later on, to be sure, Miss Johnston sometimes wandered from the ways of primness, but Thomas Nelson Page never faltered. When he died in 1923, after a distinguished career as novelist and diplomatist, he was again writing a novel of the Reconstruction, working the lucrative soil he had once before chosen in *Red Rock*. When word came of Thomas Nelson Page's death, the flag over the Capitol in Richmond flew at half-mast. Schools and colleges adjourned; kings, premiers, presidents telegraphed their messages of sympathy. For many a Virginia lady and gentleman, he was the beau ideal of all that a Southern writer and man of letters should be.

In seeking to understand and evaluate the life and work of Ellen Anderson Gholson Glasgow, then, one must not forget Thomas Nelson Page, nor that all-revealing "but" employed by his brother Rosewell in the *Library of Southern Literature*. As her friend and fellow modernist James Branch Cabell declared of Ellen Glasgow's early books, when they were written "the ghost of Thomas Nelson Page still haunted everybody's conception of the South, keening in Negro dialect over the Confederacy's fallen heroes."[7] It is all very well to point out, as I shall attempt to do, the limitations of Ellen Glasgow's "realism," to enter some reservations concerning the intensity of that blood and irony she proposed

* Though *John Marvel, Assistant* is surely a problem novel above all.

6

to apply as cure for the troubles of her native region, to suggest even that in certain respects Miss Ellen's work seems today to lie somewhat closer to the same Thomas Nelson Page than to, say, William Faulkner. It is all very well to make such observations. From the standpoint of a critical look at twentieth-century Southern literature it is even essential.

Yet all the same, in Miss Ellen's time and place the Rosewell Pages did count for something. It is one thing to write novels in the South of William Faulkner's day, and quite another to have done so in the South of Thomas Nelson and Rosewell Page.

2. Blood and Irony

"WHAT THE SOUTH MOST NEEDS," runs Ellen Glasgow's most famous literary and social pronouncement, "is blood and irony." The implication, as developed again and again in that deft set of critical prefaces entitled *A Certain Measure*, was that she had provided both. There can be no doubt that she tried very hard to do so. For the better part of forty years she devoted her literary talents to an intensive scrutiny of life in Virginia, exploring as many facets of it as she knew existed. The twelve novels in the Virginia edition of her work, and five others not included, dealt with Virginians in Virginia. Aging gentlemen of first families, young blue bloods coming to grips with the modern world, serene Episcopalian communicants, gospel-ridden fundamentalists, free thinkers, heroines of high birth and low estate, good country folk, politicians, bankers, lawyers, generals, clerks, factory workers, industrial tycoons, ministers, tobacco, peanut and wheat farmers, dairymen, ladies of the old school and women of the market place, emancipated modern girls and tradition-bound ladies of high degree, Negroes as well as whites—all these people her books. Agriculture, industry, politics, the law, medicine, finance, warfare, education, retailing, wholesaling, domestic work—her characters engaged in most of the occupations known to Virginians during the period of her renowned Social History of the Old Dominion. "I intended to treat the static customs of the country, as well as the changing provincial patterns of the small towns and cities," she wrote. "Moreover, I planned to portray the different social orders, and especially, for this would constitute the major theme of my chronicle, the rise of the middle class as the dominant force in Southern democracy."[8] Yet she would be more than the mere documentary journalist. She would look inward, showing the lonely spirits of those men and women whose lives she narrated: "We find, in a certain measure, what we have to give, if not what we seek, both in the external world about us and in the more solitary life of the mind."[9] In terms of subject matter at least, Miss Glasgow surely succeeded in this venture. As the historian C. Vann Woodward has said of her, "when eventually the bold moderns of the South arrested the reading and theatrical world with the tragic intensity of the inner life and social drama of the South, they could find scarcely a theme that Ellen Glasgow had wholly neglected."[10]

She was a realist, she declared firmly, and she believed it. She would look at the life around her with eyes unclouded by sentiment or veiled by romance. Heartily she applauded Stuart P. Sherman's remark, made in the 1920s, that "Miss Glasgow's democratic fight in realism is incarnate in the little red-haired hero of *The Voice of the People*. Realism crossed the Potomac twenty-five years ago going North." That novel, which was first published in 1900, was, so far as Miss Glasgow was aware, "the first work of genuine realism to appear in Southern fiction."*[11] If her friend James Branch Cabell tended sometimes toward the ethereal, if his "delicate pursuit of the unholy grail wears, on high occasions, the semblance of allegory,"[12] she herself would strive as always for "a downward seeking into the stillness of vision, as well as an upward springing into the animation of the external world. For the novel, and indeed every form of art, no matter how rooted it may be in a particular soil, must draw nourishment from the ancient instincts, the blood and tears, which are the common heritage of mankind."[13] And in another passage in *A Certain Measure* which both in rhetoric and content notably anticipates a famous pronouncement by William Faulkner made some years later, she stated that "the qualities which will unite to make great Southern novels are the elemental properties which make great novels wherever they are written in any part of the world: power, passion, pity, ecstasy and anguish, hope and despair."[14]

For good or ill, this was what Ellen Glasgow sought after when

* She had evidently not read George Washington Cable's *John March, Southerner* (1894). Nor have many others, either before or since.

9

she wrote her fiction, and in general it has been the verdict of most historians of American literature (though not, however, of many *critics* of American literature) that this is precisely where the achievement of her art rests. One of her earliest and most steadfast admirers, Edwin Mims, found her work admirably designed to express the firm-minded, forward-looking realism he advocated for the South. "She is a realist," he wrote, "in the sense that she shows us life as it is, life shorn of its romance and illusions, but she has also the hope, the courage, the patience and the faith of the chastened romantic and the tempered idealist." For Mims, Miss Glasgow had "a faith in democracy as real and as vital as was that of Thomas Jefferson or Walter Page." "There is not a single progressive movement in the South today," he wrote in 1926, "that may not find enlightenment and inspiration in some one of her novels."[15]

In the authoritative *Literary History of the United States,* her friend Henry Seidel Canby wrote broadly and approvingly that "she is most colorful in her early historical novels, where, with an impassioned realism, she handles the story of the Lost Cause which the sentimentalists had made into a rosy legend. She is most profound and greatest in her stories of the land. She is most subtle, most ironic, and most critical in her novels of city life."[16] And Alfred Kazin declared that "she began as the most girlish of Southern romantics and later proved the most biting critic of Southern romanticism; she was at once the most traditional in loyalty to Virginia and its most powerful satirist; the most sympathetic historian of the Southern mind in modern times and a consistent satirist of that mind. She wrote like a dowager and frequently suggested the mind of a nihilist; she was at once the most old-fashioned of contemporary American novelists and frequently the wittiest."[17] For Van Wyck Brooks, she was "the first novelist to picture the true Southern life."[18]

To this well-nigh universal historian's-eye view of Ellen Glasgow as tough-minded, objective portrayer of the essence and accidence of mortal man on Southern earth, seemingly only James

Branch Cabell, of all who knew her well, made objection. His friend was a Virginia gentlewoman, he declared, and she wrote and thought like a Virginia gentlewoman—which is to say, with more than a little romance and sentimentality about her. Archly he noted certain other than down-to-earth qualities in her work. There was a pervasive optimism and air of spiritual uplift, he remarked: "A fair number of Ellen Glasgow's characters," for example, "toward the end of their printed histories, get spiritual comfort out of observing a light in the sky or in somebody's eyes."[19] No matter how barren and cruel the vicissitudes of existence tend to become for her Virginians, Miss Glasgow still would "almost always manage to end, somehow, on the brave note of recording her people's renovated belief in a future during which everything will turn out quite splendidly." Hers was the exact note, Mr. Cabell declared, of "the last and indeed the expiring cry of romance."[20]

When Mr. Cabell suggested that deep within Miss Ellen's metaphysic there was something rather more tender than tough, when he remarked that her main theme was not blood and irony so much as "The Tragedy Of Everywoman, As It Was Lately Enacted In The Commonwealth of Virginia," he made his observation out of a more than forty-year acquaintanceship with his subject. It was a relationship that for the later portions of Miss Glasgow's life had been quite close, and even, during the writing of her last novel, approaching literary collaboration.

His various hints that Miss Glasgow's art was not wholly removed from the romantic and the subjective, and that the social history of Virginia might possibly involve consideration of the novelist herself as well as her novels, were not overly popular with Miss Glasgow's more devoted admirers, nor, we may deduce, with Miss Ellen herself. When in 1954, ten years after her death, Miss Glasgow's literary executors released for publication her secret, designedly posthumous autobiographical memoir, *The Woman Within,* it was discovered that Mr. Cabell was something less of a favorite of Miss Glasgow's than might have been thought. What she did in that work was to revive several long-forgotten near-scandals of Mr. Cabell's youth and divulge a little behind-the-scenes knowledge of Mr. Cabell's domestic habits.

Mr. Cabell, however, had the last word, and in *As I Remember It* (1955), his final book of memoirs, he tinted the portrait of his deceased friend with considerable irony, noting among other things her jealousy for reputation and her careful cultivation of all literary figures who might conceivably advance her standing, suggesting that she was not entirely above exaggerating and even fictionalizing the events of her love life, and reiterating his previous verdict, to the effect that "she remained always, during at any rate the last twenty years of her life, an unhappy woman, resentful of that which she—still sullenly, but far from tacitly—esteemed to be the outrageous unfairness of heaven's traffic with Ellen Glasgow."[21]

The decision went to Mr. Cabell, the more so because it seems fairly evident that he knew whereof he spoke. Miss Glasgow's posthumous memoir only confirmed his previous estimate of her. It bore out his basic contention, written essentially in friendship and admiration even at the last, I think, that Miss Glasgow generally depicted life through the eyes of a highly feminine, subjective percipient, one who had indeed suffered as a woman and whose work was written in large measure out of that suffering and took much of its character from it.

For the portrait of Ellen Glasgow, as seen in *The Woman Within* and her other work, is not that of a realist. It was no convert to blood and irony who wrote that "life had defrauded me of something precious that I could never recover,"[22] who could say, of a physician who commented on her seeming cheerfulness despite the deafness that had afflicted her for most of her life, that "if only he could know! If only anyone in the world could know! That I, who was winged for flying, should be wounded and caged!"[23] There could indeed be nothing more specifically romantic, for example, than Miss Glasgow's revealing description of herself as a child: "Yet I was not ever a normal child. Far and wide as the common denominator might expand, it had never benignly included me."[24]

It might have been better, for the sake of the image of herself that Ellen Glasgow sought to bequeath to the world, had she never written, or, having written, authorized the posthumous publication of, *The Woman Within.* Yet the evidence is there more importantly in her novels, where its only real significance lies. They are not the novels of a realist, but of a romanticist, a sentimentalist even. As John Edward Hardy rather bluntly put it, "Ellen Glasgow, in most of her work, is in *no way* essentially a realist. She is, in many ways, essentially a sentimentalist. No one of her novels is entirely sentimental, and she is less sentimental in her later work than in her earlier. But there is none of the novels that is entirely without sentimentality."[25] There is no one of her novels, that is, in which the world without is examined for its own sake and in its own right; and in many of her novels, including several customarily described as being among her most realistic and uncompromising work, the valuation given to persons and events by the novelist is so heavily freighted with the writer's private feminine desires and needs that the reader may find it all but impossible to accept Miss Glasgow's version of experience.

There is nothing inherently wrong about the romantic perspective, of course, but its limitations for writing "social history" are obvious. For by definition a social history must be the account of what actually happens to a society, and what it all means. The emphasis must be on the subject matter, for the sake of the subject matter. The social historian cannot become personally involved at the expense of his own satirical objectivity, for at that moment true satire becomes impossible. All of which is a way of saying that Miss Glasgow's success at applying blood and irony in pursuit of the social history of Virginia depends upon her own detachment; and too often she is not at all detached, but instead is so intensely engaged and identified with the supposed objects of irony that she can be neither ironic nor realistic. She surrenders her objectivity to the private demands of her characters; instead of creating Dorinda in *Barren Ground,* she becomes Dorinda. Or rather, it is Dorinda who ceases to be a fictional character and becomes an extension of

Miss Glasgow's own life and personality, until it is Miss Glasgow who is undergoing the experience.

It is a good rule of thumb for the Glasgow novels that whenever the author begins identifying a character's plight with her own, begins projecting her personal wishes and needs into the supposedly fictional situation, then to that extent both the character and the novel are weakened. Contrariwise, Miss Glasgow's success as a novelist is in direct proportion to her success in standing away from her characters and letting them find their own fictional level, as created figures in a story. In at least three of the novels of the Social History, when by and large she managed to do that, the result was successful fiction, successful social portraiture, and in one instance fairly close to a triumph.

In *A Certain Measure* and elsewhere, Miss Glasgow gave us to understand that her plan for writing a Social History of Virginia was reached quite early in her career—as early as 1899, in fact, when she began work on *The Voice of the People*. Here too, however, James Branch Cabell demurred. The actual title, he declares in *As I Remember It*, was his own, "for during the early summer of 1928 I reminded Ellen that, when reviewing *Barren Ground* for the *Nation*, during the May of 1925, I had expressed my large, personal admiration of the completeness with which her books, as a whole, presented a 'portrayal of social and economic Virginia since the War Between the States.'" Since Doubleday, Doran and Company were about to bring out a uniform edition of her books, Mr. Cabell suggested that Miss Glasgow should henceforth style her work accordingly. Miss Glasgow "agreed dubiously as to its possibilities," Mr. Cabell remembered, and then "enkindled to them cannily," until after a time she had completely convinced herself "that ever since 1899 she had been at work on 'a social history in the more freely interpretative form of fiction.' And equally was everybody else convinced also."*[26]

* Mr. Cabell's revelation was received by Miss Glasgow's admirers with some surprise and, in some instances, with no little indignation. H. Blair

Whether or not Miss Glasgow was consciously compiling a social history as such for all those decades, however, it is undeniably true that for all practical purposes she was writing such a history. Perhaps the conscious titling did come later, and at Mr. Cabell's prompting; nonetheless, from 1900 onward the subject matter of her novels was directed toward that end. Edwin Mims, for example, recognized this when he wrote in 1926 that Miss Glasgow "has written a series of novels that now approach a certain epic proportion by reason of their presentation of a well-defined period of history that reaches from the Civil War to the [First] World War."[28]

Yet the controversy does have some bearing on Miss Glasgow and her work, for if Mr. Cabell's contention is true, it is a prime illustration of the way Miss Glasgow's mind worked, revealing as it does a kind of rage for outward self-control, an insistence upon her own prescience and objectivity at all costs.*

Rouse, for example, in editing Miss Glasgow's *Letters* (1958), included a letter written to Allen Tate in 1933 in which she explained that her early novels "were all included in a social history of Virginia I planned long ago. For years I worked with this idea, but gave it up just before I wrote *Barren Ground*." To this passage Mr. Rouse appended a note that "this appears to contradict James Branch Cabell's assumption that he gave Miss Glasgow the idea for thinking of her work as a social history of Virginia . . ."[27] Just how it so appears is difficult to say; Mr. Cabell's whole point was that after 1928 Miss Glasgow came devoutly to believe that she had been consciously at work on a project of social history ever since 1899. If anything, absence of talk about this plan from any of the letters in Mr. Rouse's collection until those of the year 1933 would tend to substantiate Mr. Cabell's claim, it seems to me.

* Reminiscent, I might add, of another distinguished Richmond author, the historian Douglas Southall Freeman, who again and again claimed for his life work a kind of Platonic predetermination as to unswerving purpose and direction, calmly and rationally planned out so far in advance that not even Dr. Freeman, disciplined craftsman though he was, could possibly have managed it.

3. Learning To Live Without Joy

The Voice of the People was Miss Glasgow's third novel, and the first volume of the Social History. For though the hero of *The Descendant* and the heroine of *Phases of an Inferior Planet* come from Virginia, they have very little, save perhaps by inference, to do with the state. Miss Glasgow intended *The Voice of the People,* she says, as a description of "the historic drama of a changing order and the struggle of an emerging middle class. . . . The old agrarian civilization was passing; the new industrial system was but beginning to spring up from chaos."[29] The account of a poor farm boy's rise to political power, the novel deals with the effects of the increasing political control of the state by the farmers, the political and social reaction of the older classes to the new middle class, and even, vaguely, with the Negro question. Certainly in the year 1900 much of its contents must have seemed quite "realistic," even downright vulgar, to many readers. Not merely the lynching scene at the close, but such other matters as adultery, illegitimacy, a hint or two of loose sexual goings-on, conniving politicos many of whom bore honored names, a vigorous depiction of a state political convention (Miss Glasgow was always very proud of this), and a less than bucolic description of the monotony and brutality of dirt farming were unusual fare in novels by young Southern ladies. And if this is the book in which realism was supposed to have crossed the Potomac going North, it is here that the realism resides.

For all that, *The Voice of the People* is not a realistic novel. The protagonist, Nick Burr, the farm boy whose rise to political power is supposed to symbolize the rise of the white democracy to control of the state, is nobody's realistic man of the world. As a boy he is romantic, idealized, and as a man hollow and lifeless. The point of the novel depends upon Nick Burr's becoming a martyr to truth, progress, and democratic ideals, and Nick Burr is not real enough to be a martyr to anything. The truth is that beyond a general notion that Nick was to signify the best element of the new democracy, Miss Glasgow had no real notion of what Nick Burr meant—nor, beyond the level of the pat abstraction, of what the new democracy meant. Nick's fate in the novel illustrates this failure. Miss Glasgow could not figure out exactly how or why Nick Burr was supposed to introduce the new democratic ideals to Virginia, because she did not know what the new ideals, if any, were. So the only conclusion she could find for Nick Burr's career, once she had elected him governor and was forced to make good on his idealism, was to have him shot to death while attempting to save a Negro from being lynched. This *deus-ex-machina* ending was in fact no solution at all. The result is that the highly romantic love story, about which the political and social portrayal is entwined, is allowed to dominate the novel, and Nicholas Burr, instead of being the embodiment of the middle class rising to political power and economic independence, remains primarily the jilted lover, first of a long line of such, male and female, in Miss Glasgow's work.

Miss Glasgow was never quite able to solve this problem of exactly what the new democracy meant for Virginia life. At the end of her career she was given to a general indictment of modernity, though on ethical rather than political grounds. Before then, however, she tried once more to explain the meaning of the new democracy, in *One Man in His Time* (1922), supposedly the last of the "transition" novels that came before she found her true artistic account in *Barren Ground*. In terms of technique, *One Man in His Time* is a considerably more subtle work than *The Voice of the People*, though it suffers grievously from some highly melodramatic plotting.

It too depicts a member of the rising middle class, one Gideon Vetch, as he seeks to introduce democratic government and high ideals into Virginia political life, to the consternation of the political bosses and the social aristocracy alike. This time Miss Glasgow decided to base her narrative not directly on Gideon, but as he is seen by Stephen Culpeper. This scion of Richmond aristocracy be-

17

comes increasingly respectful of Gideon Vetch's character and ideals as the novel develops, as well as increasingly enamoured of his daughter Patty. When Vetch decides to dispense with his corrupt political allies and take his case to the people, he, like Nick Burr, is confronted with a problem which was basic for Miss Glasgow as critic of society—how to fuse abstract ideals with actual political democracy in Virginia. Once again the sole solution Miss Glasgow could find was to kill off Vetch: he is accidentally shot during a political convention.

The only meaning that Miss Glasgow could discover for Vetch lay in some sort of vague "union," or fusion of discordant elements. "He was the only one who could have held us together," one of his supporters declares. "In touching him we touched a humanity that is as rare as genius itself," says one of his erstwhile foes, a judge of noble lineage. Another member of the aristocracy, Corinna Page, who had fallen in love with Vetch, thinks to herself that "they had killed him because they could not understand him!" Which at any rate is certainly what his creator had done.

The most effective portions of *One Man in His Time* come during some of the reveries of Stephen Culpeper, who when thinking about the mores of Queensborough society and not about high political ideals manages to provide some provocative insights into a particular subject which later on became the focus of Miss Glasgow's best work—the aristocracy faced with defining its own shrinking function in the face of increasing middle-class infiltration. Unfortunately Gideon Vetch himself has little to do with this; he represents only a hazy kind of cohesive political quality, never quite explained. The situation, indeed, foreshadows a later Southern novel, Robert Penn Warren's *All the King's Men*. Maxwell Geismar has noted this, too.[30] The difference is that Willie Stark of that novel is killed off at the close not because his creator could not discover a meaning for him, but because his assassination has a very definite meaning: the collapse of an unnatural, pragmatic, social fusion which cannot hold a society together. Where Willie Stark's downfall means everything to his aristocratic aide, Jack Burden,

18

Gideon Vetch's demise means for Stephen Culpeper only that a kind of vague idealistic force has been removed from the scene—and that Patty Vetch is bereaved.

As previously noted, the genuine insights in *One Man in His Time,* as well as in *The Voice of the People,* lie not in the political symbolism, which is always cloudy, but in the problem of social class. What Miss Glasgow excels in is the occasional moment in which a member of the First Families of Virginia confronts someone of lower status in a situation that has social implications. At such times Miss Glasgow more often than not senses the problems of definition that are involved and presents them with real understanding. One is reminded of Lionel Trilling's account of the novel as having been born in response to snobbery, "with the appearance of money as a social element—money, the great solvent of the solid fabric of a social element, the great generator of illusion." Snobbery, as Mr. Trilling reminds us, "is not the same thing as pride of class," but instead is "pride in status without pride of function. . . . The dominant emotions of snobbery are uneasiness, self-consciousness, self-defensiveness, the sense that one is not quite real but can in some way acquire reality."[31]

Surely the best elements of Miss Glasgow's work draw directly on such a theme. This aspect of the Social History is convincingly genuine—if not always in Miss Glasgow's interpretations themselves, then at least in what we perceive while watching Miss Glasgow as she interprets.

One of the most successful of the very early novels, *The Miller of Old Church* (1911), is based squarely on this theme of the function of class, without the banalities of political application that so mar *The Voice of the People.* Jonathan Gay, highborn young dilettante come back to south-side Virginia, struggles throughout the novel to attain some sort of equilibrium in the nonaristocratic community that surrounds him, but he cannot effect the transition. At the last he dies, for he and his ideas and attitudes have no more validity in the milieu where he must live.

Abel Revercomb, the miller who finally gets the girl, is one of

Miss Glasgow's more revealing characterizations. It is with increasing fascination that one watches Miss Glasgow attempting to make him emotionally, which is to say socially, worthy of marriage to Molly Merryweather. He begins as an industrious but rather stolid and prosaic rustic, a Good, Sturdy Yeoman, while Molly Merryweather begins as the tempestuous, orphaned, "complex" child of love, whose mother was of plain country stock but whose father was of the squirearchy. She, of course, is of the common folk by lot and station, but by her father's blood and temperament an aristocrat. At first Abel is simply too dull for Molly, for all his sturdy integrity. Later on she inherits money and her station, too, becomes elevated, but in the interim she supposedly realizes that the good Abel is her true desire, thus choosing a clean life of honest toil with the humble miller rather than one of aristocratic dissipation in her own class. However, as Maxwell Geismar remarks,* Molly's "most attractive traits were derived from her illegitimate connection with an old planter family."[33] And what Miss Glasgow really sets out energetically to do, throughout the novel, is not to make Molly worthy of Abel, so much as to make Abel sufficiently imaginative for Molly to find him satisfactory as a partner. At the close of the novel, Jonathan Gay, Molly's far-from-disinterested cousin, is shot to death, as if to eliminate any possibility of Molly's backsliding, and Molly and the miller are united. The miller has in the meantime installed up-to-date milling equipment in his mill, gained political success, and also married and then lost a wife, suffering cruelly all the while, thus taking on considerably more stature and subtlety

* Primarily in order to demonstrate that Miss Glasgow was still quite a snob. Elsewhere Geismar declares that "what's odd is not that [the belief in caste and class] should dominate the romantic Southern literature of the 1900s, as in the novels of Thomas Nelson Page or Thomas Dixon, but that even here, in a mind which was essentially rational, critical, ironic, and in open revolt against this tradition, it should still pervade and color the writings of Ellen Glasgow herself for so long a period."[32] It is just barely possible that Miss Glasgow's mind was *not* so essentially rational, critical, ironic as all that (Mr. Geismar wrote without benefit of *The Woman Within*, but the novels were there as evidence) and also that a feeling for social complexity is not necessarily alien and opposed to intelligent thought.

while losing some of his sturdy, yeoman simplicity. Even so, the end of the book is unconvincing; one doesn't really concede that Molly is quite ready to wed and bed with Abel Revercomb, for all of Miss Glasgow's valiant attempts to prepare us for the union. It is fortunate perhaps that Molly is, after all, still the child of unwed parents, and also that, with Jonathan's death, she inherits the family fortune, so that her marriage with the miller may not mean that she will be forced to give up her recently acquired upper-class luxury.

One is tempted to read Miss Glasgow's personal concerns into this situation. It is most interesting, for example, to realize that, particularly in Miss Glasgow's early work, whenever a heroine contemplates marriage, the problem is usually one of whether to wed *beneath* her social station, or not to wed at all. And to speculate as to exactly what that situation meant for a highly intelligent, and also highly romantic, young Virginia woman growing up in an increasingly nonfunctional, anachronistic aristocratic society, is rather intriguing, even if somewhat extraliterary. In *The Woman Within* she tells of being "eager for gaiety" as a young girl, of being "light and graceful on my feet, a natural dancer," but being, even at the age of seventeen, "still ignorant of what we call, euphemistically, 'the facts of life.' " She speaks of having "found myself neglected by the Virginia Military Institute, in Lexington; but . . . at Mr. Jefferson's University, I was not ever a wallflower, I was, indeed, a brilliant success." Yet when she goes on to describe that success, it appears to have consisted in large measure of being allowed, privately, to take and pass with distinction an examination in economics![34] Thereafter she declined the customary coming-out party in Richmond society, and from then on her mind was turned toward matters of the intellect.

Her closest affection and strongest admiration seems to have been for Walter McCormack, the husband of her sister Cary, "a sound and brilliant thinker." Her first novel, *The Descendant*, was dedicated to him. Miss Glasgow's grief over his untimely death by suicide while only twenty-six years of age was overwhelming. "No one who has not lived with a broken heart, hour by hour, day by day, week by week, month by month, year by year, can know what the next two or three years meant in this house," she wrote, ostensibly speaking only of her sister's grief. She remarks, too, that "Walter had been fond of me; we had understood each other; and I was the only person who could feel and know why he had chosen the one way of escape."[35] (One thinks of certain aspects of *The Sheltered Life*.) Miss Glasgow seems certainly never to have encountered any eligible male of her own social circle in Richmond whose intellect and temperament were akin to hers; and, as Mr. Cabell reminds us, so far as Richmond society was concerned Miss Glasgow was not remotely a social egalitarian.

In *Virginia*, the novel that followed *The Miller of Old Church*, the heroine did not marry beneath herself. Rather, Virginia Pendleton Treadwell was wed to someone considerably her intellectual superior, so that the plot of the novel becomes one of a sweet, well-intentioned, "old-fashioned" girl attempting, and ultimately failing, to achieve a satisfactory marriage with a brooding, eccentric modern, a dramatist who sacrifices his high artistic standards to the economic demands of home and family, and then after he becomes a prosperous, popular playwright deserts his wife for an actress. So we have another interesting problem, but with the roles reversed —and significantly, I think, we have the novel of Ellen Glasgow's which, next to the three comedies of her later life, is by far the most successful fiction.

Miss Glasgow called *Virginia* "the first book of my maturity." One can agree wholeheartedly. "Virginia was more than a woman," she said: "she was the embodiment of a forsaken ideal":[36]

And like my mother, Virginia, who was the perfect flower of Southern culture, was educated according to the simple theory that the less a girl knew about life, the better prepared she would be to contend with it. "The chief object of her upbringing, which differed in no essential particular from that of every other well-bred and well-born Southern woman of her day, was to paralyze her reasoning faculties so completely that all danger of mental unsettling, or even movement, was eliminated from her future." Love comes, as fleeting as ecstasy, and her strength, for she is not weak in fibre, hardens into the inherited emotional patterns.[37]

Maxwell Geismar is properly appreciative of this characterization, and hails the passage in the novel from which Miss Glasgow quoted as "major writing, of course, brilliant and perceptive. . . . You begin to realize that the 'inherited mould of fixed beliefs' was even more impressive in the small towns of the South than in the nineteenth-century New England or those bustling western towns that Sinclair Lewis was to immortalize a few years later."[38] Fine writing some of it is, and what Mr. Geismar says about oppressive customs and fixed beliefs may well have been true—but, as we shall see, there is a significant alteration in Miss Glasgow's valuation of Virginia as the narrative proceeds.

Virginia is a novel involving numerous problems of social transition. Not only the intellectual in the Virginia community, but the relationship of the tobacco magnate to that community, the double-standard attitude of the South toward racial mores, the efficacy of genteel education in an increasingly commercialized society are closely bound with the plot of the novel. Its relative success as a work of fiction, however, lies not in this, but in the characterization of the heroine. For almost alone of Miss Glasgow's protagonists up to that time, Virginia is very much a creature of limitation. Miss Glasgow set out to draw a typical Virginia woman of the old school, born into a world where the traditional standards of conduct were becoming more and more inadequate. Virginia, therefore, does not, consciously at any rate, speak for Miss Glasgow; the author does not project her own personality into her character's. She saw Virginia as a contained, bounded person of just so much sensibility and imagination. It was as if Miss Glasgow attempted to depict the kind of gentlewoman *she* herself was not—and because she understood her, succeeded.

Yet was Virginia so very foreign to her creator's own personality? One is not so sure, especially after reading *The Woman Within.*

Miss Glasgow tells us in *A Certain Measure* that "although, in the beginning, I had intended to deal ironically with both the Southern lady and Victorian tradition, I discovered, as I went on, that my irony grew fainter, while it yielded at last to sympathetic compassion."[39] Virginia does indeed grow in attractiveness and in the reader's sympathy as the novel develops. The characterization is sure, discerning, believable. Her husband Oliver, the playwright, may seem farfetched and not very credible at times; Oliver's uncle, the industrialist Cyrus Treadwell, may at times seem a mere caricature of the *nouveau-riche* exploiter and materialist; but Miss Glasgow's handling of her heroine is firm and positive from the start. Virginia convincingly symbolizes the well-born, "old-fashioned" girl who moves deeper and deeper into bewilderment as she strives in vain to adjust her instincts and her upbringing to a modern world in which old values and beliefs are less and less operative. Yet the reader's sympathies are ever more closely engaged with her, and one is by no means convinced at the close that Virginia's own values, outmoded though they may be, are therefore unworthy. Rather, one comes to feel—and evidently Miss Glasgow did too—that it may well be the times, and not Virginia, that are out of joint. This is what Mr. Geismar did not concede, for his sympathies are ever with the modern rather than the traditional.

I do not say that Virginia is Ellen Glasgow; not at all. Indeed, Miss Glasgow certainly believed her character was everything that she herself was not. But I do feel that for all of Miss Glasgow's devotion to irony and emancipation, there was always a great deal of Virginia in her emotional make-up, and so there is a part of Miss Glasgow in Virginia—the part, that is, that she knew and recognized in the life about her, and which was not enough for her. But it was enough for Virginia, and in seeing her as a finite, bounded person, Miss Glasgow was able to achieve a convincing, harmonious characterization. The Virginia in herself she knew and understood very well, even if she did not perceive how much of it was always there, or how important it was. The other side of Miss Glasgow's personality, the part that she did recognize within herself, the part that made her break away and rebel, the part, that is, that produced the novelist of ideas instead of the housewife, Miss Glasgow did not understand nearly so well. And when that part of her got into her fiction, her troubles began.

We see this clearly, I believe, in *Barren Ground* (1925), Miss Glasgow's favorite of her novels, her self-confessed masterpiece. "What I saw, as my novel unfolded," she wrote, "was a complete reversal of a classic situation. For once, in Southern fiction, the betrayed woman would become the victor instead of the victim."[40] In her autobiography she declared that "I wrote *Barren Ground*, and immediately I knew I had found myself."[41] And again, "when I began *Barren Ground*, I knew that I had found a code of living that was sufficient for life or for death."[42] Miss Glasgow's high valuation of the novel was largely shared by its reviewers when it appeared in 1925. Among them was James Branch Cabell, who as late as 1947 still considered it "to have been the most important of my dear friend's novels."*[43]

Dorinda Oakley, the central figure of *Barren Ground*, is a farm girl who is betrayed in her love for Jason Greylock, a young man of higher caste but weaker will. Dorinda proceeds to rise above it. She flees to New York, earns a living there for a while, then comes home and converts her father's run-down dirt farm into a prosperous commercial dairy operation. She extends her holdings, is married—though not for love—to an honest storekeeper who later dies a hero in a train wreck, and as the novel closes, she has achieved what is represented as a satisfying life.

Dorinda's chief virtue, as Miss Glasgow frequently informs us, is her integrity and courage. " 'We'll stay here alone, Ma and I,' Dorinda declared, with the stern integrity she had won from transgression." Again, "strange how her courage had revived with the sun! . . . for the vital spirit and the eager mind, the future will

* Though in 1956, in an interview with the present writer, Mr. Cabell entered a significant reservation: "I think I like *The Romantic Comedians* and *They Stooped To Folly* best, although *Barren Ground* was probably her best book. I didn't enjoy it so much, myself."[44]

always hold the search for buried treasure and the possibilities of high adventure. . . . At middle age she faced the future without romantic glamour, but she faced it with integrity of vision." Miss Glasgow greatly admired the heroine of *Barren Ground*. Dorinda was, she declares in a revealing description, "universal. She exists wherever a human being has learned to live without joy, wherever the spirit of fortitude has triumphed over the sense of futility."[45]

In just what, exactly, does Dorinda's vaunted courage reside? Supposedly it lies in her decision, after her unfortunate love affair with the well-to-do Jason Greylock, to turn her back on all those things which as a girl she most desires—love, affection, sexual fulfillment, a husband and family. When in love with Jason Greylock she had used some of her hard-won savings to purchase a blue dress, because Jason had suggested that she should wear blue. Riding to church in the blue dress, "she felt that joy mounted in her veins as the sap flowed upward about her." For the remainder of her post-romantic life she gave no further thought to blue dresses. In essence, Dorinda's courage consists of learning to live without the blue dress, "to live without joy." What Dorinda does, once the love affair has ended in disillusion, is to spend her days denying her femininity, refusing to indulge herself as a woman. She will be as hard, as unromantic, as business minded as any man; from then on, all notions of living as a human being with the accustomed human consolations of love, marriage, a family, are steadily driven from her mind. Her triumph is one of superhuman self-sufficiency over human dependence and weakness.

It is a triumph, most of all, of sterility. For *Barren Ground* is an aptly named novel. Dorinda's life is a progressive espousal of barrenness. She is not fruitful. As a woman she fears, abhors sexual love. As a farmer she converts the land from agriculture to pasture for commercial dairying operations. Her father, though beaten by the land, loved it; Dorinda sees it as a commodity. As a human being, Dorinda is alive only during the brief interval when she is in love, "as the sap flowed upward about her," suffering, resisting her loveless fate. Otherwise she is lifeless, impersonal.

What is most unsatisfactory about the novel is the lack of any believable motivation for the characters. Jason Greylock's weakening, his betrayal of Dorinda whom he loves, and his progressive deterioration afterward, are blamed on fate; there is no real reason why he should so decline, any more than there is any real reason why the land should defeat him and leave him homeless and exhausted. Dorinda's husband Nathan dies a hero in a train wreck, but nothing he has done or been in his life makes his death the heroic act it is supposed to be, for as a person he has never been sufficiently alive for the reader to care very much whether he lives or dies. Above all, Dorinda's choice of the joyless existence is unbelievable; her lifeless knuckling under to a kind of Thomas Hardy-like fate, symbolized by the Wessex-style broom sedge that adorns the novel, has no adequate basis in her personality. Miss Glasgow means it to be a passionate decision, but it seems peculiarly cold-blooded and inhuman. Dorinda gives in to fate, becomes a sexless automaton.

In what way this constitutes true courage, as Miss Glasgow insists, one is hard put to say. The courageous act might have been for Dorinda to refuse to give in to misfortune, to persist in being her own passionate self and to hew to her own true nature in defiance of all fate or misfortune. This she does not do; after one unsuccessful attempt to find love amid the broom sedge, she yields to her fate. Above all she had wanted to be a woman, to love and be loved, to make of the broom sedge a garden. Instead she converts it into a commercial dairy farm.

The result is a book remarkable most of all for its spiritual barrenness. Miss Glasgow meant it for a vindication of the life of stern, emotion-denying fortitude and repudiation of human weakness. What she achieved was a novel in which vitality, whether of character or of landscape, is singularly absent. In writing *Barren Ground*, we remember, she felt that she had "found a code of living that was sufficient for life or for death." One agrees, ironically. For as a living, feeling, believable human being, Dorinda ceases to exist once her romantic moment is done. Spiritually, dramatically, she is thereafter dead. It has not been a vindication that has taken place, but an indictment.

In *The Woman Within,* Miss Glasgow more than once summed up what she considered her own essential courage:

> Always I have had to learn for myself, from within. Always I have persevered in the face of an immense disadvantage—in the face of illness, or partial deafness, which came later, to blaze my own trail through the wilderness that was ignorance. To teach one's self is to be forced to learn twice. Yet, no doubt it is true, as my friends assure me, that when one hews out from rock a personality or an understanding it stays fast in the mind. Only a hunger and thirst for knowledge can bring perseverance.[46]

Now there is no doubt that this is precisely the way that Miss Glasgow thought of Dorinda. One need only substitute for *knowledge* the words *emotional independence,* as Miss Glasgow so often did, and we have an apt characterization of what Miss Glasgow claimed for the heroine of *Barren Ground,* that farm woman who at middle age "faced the future without romantic glamour, but . . . faced it with integrity of vision." Then why does the heroine of *Barren Ground* seem so lifeless and without humanity, when her admiring creator herself was in many ways so very feminine, so very human and attractive a person?

The answer is simply that Miss Glasgow only *thought* she was like Dorinda Oakley; in actuality she was much more. She did indeed possess more than her share of "integrity of vision," of firm, Presbyterian resolve to hold to her course in spite of all obstacles. But as a person—we have the novels for witness, and we have *The Woman Within*—she also possessed a great deal of what she made Dorinda Oakley deny: the craving for love, for romance, for affection, for acclaim. Her own personality, her growing deafness, her intellectual interests in a community not, as James Branch Cabell has remarked, overly sympathetic to such interests, seems somehow to have denied her all but literary acclaim. And for fame, as her *Letters* and Mr. Cabell's reminiscences alike show, she was always most zealous. In Mr. Cabell's words, "she wanted also—or rather, she tacitly and sullenly demanded of heaven, I think—as an atoning for the normal pleasures and the normal ties and the normal contacts with her fellow beings which circumstances had denied her, fame and daily applause."[47] Around her Ellen Glasgow collected a noted circle indeed of reviewers, critics, scholars, journalists who, as Mr. Cabell enviously noted, basked in the radiance of her personality, and then went home to write about it.*

Far from being the Spartan woman, then, Ellen Glasgow seems to have yearned eagerly all her life for what she insisted Dorinda Oakley had absolutely no need of—love, admiration, affection. And in this respect we recognize not Dorinda, but that much more believable Glasgow heroine, Virginia Pendleton Treadwell. For as we have seen, the personality that could write *The Woman Within* is most of all like Virginia—feminine, eager for love, in no way reconciled to a joyless, passionless, stoical life.

If it was spiritual self-portrait, then, that Ellen Glasgow consciously or unconsciously meditated in *Barren Ground,* as it so clearly seems, her effort at self-understanding was a failure. She saw but a part of herself, and thought it was all. The dimension missing from the characterization of Dorinda Oakley is that which is essential to successful characterization in fiction—human limitation, human compassion, human "ecstasy and anguish, hope and despair." And in denying the legitimate existence of all these qualities in the make-up of Dorinda Oakley, Miss Glasgow created a character both less and more than human.

Thus once again the Social History is discernible not only in the

* Toward the close of *The Woman Within,* for example, she listed those whose "friendships are enduring."[48] Among the nine persons, with their wives, so signaled out, there were numbered prominent representatives of the book-review sections of the New York *Times* and *Herald Tribune,* the *New Republic,* the *Saturday Review of Literature,* the New York *Post,* the *American Mercury;* two of the day's most eminent middle-brow literary historians, Van Wyck Brooks and Howard Mumford Jones; and Mr. Carl van Vechten. Mr. Cabell's comments on all this are to be found in his last book, *As I Remember It* (pp. 228–30).

novel, but in the picture of Miss Glasgow writing the novel. For
we remember Mr. Cabell's remarks about "The Tragedy Of Everywoman, As It Was Lately Enacted In The Commonwealth Of
Virginia." Mr. Cabell's summation of the heroine of *Barren
Ground,* and of its author, is to the point, in a sense that he did not
exactly intend: "The experiences which, by every known rule of
romantic Southern tradition, ought to have mattered most poign-
antly have, in reality, 'meant nothing.' "[49] Dorinda's supposedly
triumphant life has meant, at the last, very little. And Miss Glasgow, one might well say, sometimes felt that way herself. The picture that illumines the Social History at this point is that of the
gentlewoman in Virginia, alone and lonely in an unchivalrous age,
gritting her teeth.

4. The Great Lady

AT THE VERY CLOSE OF *Barren Ground*, after Dorinda has buried the husband she never loved and turned her vision resolutely toward the future, it is suggested to her that she may sometime wish to marry again. Thereupon Dorinda smiles, "and her smile was pensive, ironic, and infinitely wise. 'Oh, I've finished with all that,' she rejoined. 'I am thankful to have finished with all that.' " With that the novel closes.

If Dorinda was finished with all that, however, the same was not true of Miss Glasgow as a novelist. Her next three books deal directly and often humorously with the ironies of love, marriage, and procreation. Her heroes and heroines are all members of upper-level Richmond society, and the situations are directly drawn out of what is always Miss Glasgow's most successful and effective medium: social satire, the aging aristocracy in a world turning steadily more bourgeois, its members searching unsuccessfully for something to compensate for the loss of the heroic possibility. No longer is Miss Glasgow seeking to find strength and meaning in the new democracy, or to build pastoral whereby she may draw the spirit of fortitude and self-reliance from the earth folk. For three books, her best books, she eschews the heroic. Her art is restrained, serene, comic.

Perhaps the widespread popular and critical success of *Barren Ground* provided a kind of catharsis, whereby for a decade its author's psyche was drained of the anxieties and conflicts that had brought it and its immediate predecessors into being. Miss Glasgow's summary of the aftermath of that book's publication is conducive to this interpretation:

I wrote *Barren Ground,* and immediately I knew I had found myself. Recognition, so long delayed, increased with each book. After more than twenty-one years, I was at last free. If falling in love could

31

be bliss, I discovered, presently, that falling out of love could be blissful tranquillity. I had walked from a narrow overheated place out into the bracing autumnal light of the world. Earth wore, yet once again, its true colors. People and objects resumed their natural proportions.[50]

Miss Glasgow is discussing not only the aftermath of the novel but also the end of a romance with one "Harold S——." The combined description is so perfect a summation of her literary career at the time, that one remembers Mr. Cabell's remark that "her writing and the applause of her writing were the sole matters which concerned Ellen Glasgow vitally."[51] She had won fame; she had, in *Barren Ground*, "expressed herself"—to her own satisfaction at any rate. She had written a novel about a woman who was defiantly superior to all need for joy, and now proceeded joyfully to write three novels about people who were not so fortunate.

Once again, as in *Virginia*, Miss Glasgow considered herself to be above the peccadilloes and frailties of her characters, and because she saw them as limited creatures, wrote stories with believable, reasonably complete characterizations. The dominant tone is ironical, accompanied by much compassion. There is seldom the feeling that the author is identifying with the protagonists of the three novels, that her own needs are being projected into the concerns of her people. Like Dorinda Oakley, Miss Glasgow as author is "pensive, ironic, and infinitely wise," and as her characters become enmeshed in the toils of sex and love, she is mostly amused. As Edward Wagenknecht remarks, this was the period during which she was closest to James Branch Cabell, whose customary spoofing of romance in his books was a far cry from Miss Glasgow's previous attitude toward such matters. Now Miss Glasgow began to "view sex, in the Cabell manner, as furnishing the stuff of high comedy, a rare achievement in women's work."[52] Her protagonists are in turn an elderly judge, a middle-aged lawyer, and an adolescent girl. Together with the much earlier *Virginia*, these novels represent, I feel, Miss Glasgow's most successful fiction.

The central character of *The Romantic Comedians* (1926), Judge

Gamaliel Bland Honeywell, is something of a new departure in the roster of Miss Glasgow's protagonists. Having missed romance all his life, he attempts at the age of sixty-five to capture it, only to realize dimly at the close that one cannot turn back the clock. In certain respects the situation in *The Romantic Comedians* is reminiscent of earlier Glasgow novels. The protagonist cannot find love, and must learn to do without it. Love is only for lesser breeds —the youthful, insensitive Annabel, the irresponsible, heedless Mrs. Bredalbane. The Judge and Amanda Lightfoot, the sweetheart of his youth who never married, are doomed by their roles in society to live lives of circumspect dignity, without passion.

The essential difference between *The Romantic Comedians* and the earlier novels is that while Miss Glasgow does tend to take Amanda Lightfoot's plight rather seriously, Amanda remains a minor character, and Miss Glasgow does not build her novel around her. The emphasis is on the Judge, whose case is not seen as tragic; the sixty-five-year-old Judge's need of romance tends to be viewed ironically. He knows he shouldn't really marry Annabel; the merry chase she thereupon leads him is not surprising. At the close the Judge gives her up peaceably, bowing to the inevitable. Had he been a younger man, it would have mattered more, but as it is, the element of sexual passion is so little in the picture that there is no feeling that the Judge is being too cruelly punished for his sins. Miss Glasgow is ironic but compassionate, and so is the reader, yet so deftly has the characterization been realized that we simply accept the Judge for what he is, without feeling greatly outraged that things are not otherwise.

They Stooped To Folly (1929) is also built around an aging male protagonist. Virginius Curle Littlepage, a middle-aged Queensborough lawyer, is a fallible and human man, and in proportion to his fallibility, we like him. He is married to a high-minded and virtuous lady, and he has a high-minded and virtuous daughter. He dreams of romantic passion, and is attracted to a neighbor, Mrs. Dalrymple, a comely and not so high-minded woman. We wish he would gather up nerve enough to have the affair with Mrs. Dalrymple that he desires, and once he almost does, but we understand it when he cannot finally do so, because Virginius is a contained, bounded creature, and Miss Glasgow intended him to be. The sensibilities of the protagonist are admirably fitted to the requirements of the story.

In this novel too there are certain familiar motifs. Indeed, the plot situation at the beginning is all too familiar: one Milly Burden has been loved and been betrayed by a man, and issue is expected. But in *They Stooped To Folly* it transpires that the novel is not to be about Milly's fight for mastery over fate. Instead, Milly more or less fades from the scene, and nobody seems too much concerned over her woes—not even Milly. The ensuing story is a satire of manners, with Virginius Littlepage busily trying to settle his daughter Mary Victoria's troubles with her husband, Milly's erstwhile seducer, even while becoming involved in a few of his own. Unlike many another Glasgow protagonist, Virginius is less inclined to rock back and dumbly and achingly accept the buffetings of life. He tries, unsuccessfully, it is true, but nevertheless quite manfully, to do things.

The novel is not a flawless creation. Milly's early problems are out of balance in relationship to the form of the novel; and though rendered technically possible by the plot, her former lover's meeting with and ensuing marriage to Mary Victoria Littlepage seem too coincidental. A more serious flaw is the ultimate role of Louise Goddard, close friend of Virginius Littlepage's wife. At the close of the novel, after Virginius has become a widower, he learns that all her life Louise has loved and idolized him. The revelation is supposed to be quite pathetic, but it is not suited to the nature of the story Miss Glasgow is telling. Rather, the book should have closed with Virginius's ironic realization that by dying when she did his good and sterling wife had once again come between him and passion—he was perilously close to an affair with Mrs. Dalrymple when the news of his wife's demise came. As it is, the announcement of Louise Goddard's long-unrequited passion ends the book on a familiar note in Miss Glasgow's work: the woman without love, bearing her cross bravely. Dramatically this is a distraction; the meaning of the novel resides in Virginius Littlepage, and should have been allowed to remain there.

Nonetheless, *They Stooped To Folly* is for the most part effective social satire, well justifying Miss Glasgow's conviction that from the outset it was "endowed with vitality and movement."[53] If the novel itself seems at times to bear little relationship to what Miss Glasgow says about it in *A Certain Measure,* it is a deftly handled satire of morals and manners, and Virginius Littlepage must occupy a high rank among Ellen Glasgow's more impressive achievements.

Miss Glasgow's next novel was her triumph. *The Sheltered Life* is, I believe, her finest book. More than any of her other novels, even *The Romantic Comedians,* it is a formal success, with characterization, plot development, and, above all, the tone of the prose working in near-flawless harmony to produce a little masterpiece of sensibility. It was evidently a novel which was a dramatic unit from the beginning, and its meaning was evident to Miss Glasgow in the very form itself.

Maxwell Geismar notes the rather ambiguous description that Miss Glasgow gave of its inception.[54] The background, she said, was that of her childhood, but she could recall no "definite beginning or voluntary act of creation." At one moment there was "a mental landscape without figures; the next moment, as if they had been summoned by the stroke of a bell, all the characters trooped in together, with every contour, every feature, every attitude, every gesture and expression, complete."[55] The theme is that of a young girl's progression from innocence to human complicity. It is set in Richmond, during the period and in the actual neighborhood of Miss Glasgow's own childhood. The removal in time and in age— Miss Glasgow was in her fifties when she wrote it—helped to make it possible for her to create a feminine protagonist whom she felt no necessity to imbue with her own adult personality. Jenny Blair Archbald's sensibilities are effectively shaped to the requirements of the adolescent characterization. The reader not only sees what

Jenny Blair sees, but sees her as well, and she is a thoroughly believable person.

In *A Certain Measure,* Miss Glasgow declared that the central character of *The Sheltered Life* was not Jenny Blair, but her grandfather, old General Archbald, and she congratulated "at least one critic" for recognizing this.*[56] The argument is based primarily upon the importance given to a long reverie on the General's part, during which he thinks of the passage of time, his own largely restless, unsatisfied life, the increasing out-of-jointedness of the world, and the fragmented, ephemeral nature of human experience. As Miss Glasgow says, the General represents in a certain measure the lot of the "civilized man in a world that is not civilized."[58] The drive of his granddaughter Jenny Blair Archbald toward passionate involvement in human desire represents something of a fated, explosive action in which she seems almost helpless in the bonds of mortal sensuality.

It is true that at the close it is General Archbald who perceives this. Even so, the General's presence in the novel is not essential to its meaning for the reader; Jenny Blair is the seat of action and meaning, and the novel is centered directly in her growth. We watch her first childish admiration for her philandering neighbor George Birdsong, and her instinctive dissimulation of that admiration by pretending, to herself most of all, that it is George's docile wife Eva whom she most loves. Then when she is older, her attraction to George swiftly becomes conscious love, and George, being a weak soul, finally returns it in spite of himself. Whereupon the long-suffering Eva Birdsong shoots her husband to death. Jenny Blair then "began to scream with the thin, sharp cry of an animal caught in a trap." The General comforts her. " 'Oh, Grandfather, I didn't mean anything,' she cried, as she sank down into

* This was probably J. Donald Adams of the New York *Times.* But to judge from a letter from Miss Glasgow to Mr. Adams written when the book appeared, the chances are that Miss Glasgow, who as Mr. Cabell has pointed out was most skillful at this sort of thing, had carefully planted this notion in Mr. Adams's head before he wrote his review.[57]

blackness. 'I didn't mean anything in the world!' " Though it is the General who realizes how ironic, and how pathetic, are Jenny Blair's words, it is Jenny Blair who speaks them, and their meaning is applicable primarily to Jenny Blair.

The Sheltered Life is essentially a keen and sympathetic study of a young girl becoming a woman. Indeed, the murder at the close was unnecessary, even a bit overly dramatic. Eva Birdsong's action was uncharacteristic; her final rebellion against her lot tends somewhat to draw attention away from where it should have rested, on Jenny Blair's humiliation and shame at having been caught in the act. It is her story. Eva Birdsong, interesting woman though she is, is not the protagonist, any more than is General Archbald.

The General's true role in the novel, it seems to me, is to provide a kind of thematic and dramatic counterpoint for Jenny Blair. She is too young to know what she is doing; he is too old to be able to act. His way of life has closed, and hers is all new and without any precedent for her to follow. Surely this is one of the most significant perceptions of the Social History; for what Jenny Blair Archbald basically represents is a well-born young woman, raised "traditionally" and with all the old romantic illusions carefully nurtured in her, suddenly come face to face with reality. Nothing she has been told or taught is of any real use to her in coping with it. Whatever may happen in the future, she is now on her own. The General's wisdom, that of the past, cannot serve as guide or model. She will have to discover her own way.

Miss Glasgow provides this insight without being either sentimental or smug. Jenny Blair is a thoroughly motivated, quite convincing character. So, for that matter, is General Archbald, and so are the supporting characters. One wonders what will happen to Jenny Blair. It is just possible, it seems to me, that she will retreat into herself; perhaps she may even become a novelist.

5. The Women Without

THERE IS A MOMENT in *The Sheltered Life* when Jenny Blair Archbald overhears her widowed mother attempting to comfort a loveless maiden aunt, who late one night is weeping over her plight. "At least you've had love," the aunt tells Jenny Blair's mother. "You've had love, even if you lost it." Whereupon "Mrs. Archbald sighed. 'Yes, I've had love, but love isn't everything.'

'It is all I want. It is the only thing in the world I want!' "

It is a comic moment, and Miss Glasgow plays it to the full. The dialogue between the maiden aunt and Jenny Blair's mother, with Jenny Blair listening surreptitiously all the while, is a skillfully handled episode. What is remarkable is that the same woman who wrote *Barren Ground* and *Vein of Iron* could have written those lines. In that shift of attitude, while it lasted, lies the success of Miss Glasgow's three satires of manners.

Nothing so deft as that takes place in either *Vein of Iron* or *In This Our Life*, Miss Glasgow's last two novels. For after *The Sheltered Life* she turned back to her earlier high seriousness, and while in certain matters of technique the last novels are quite superior to Miss Glasgow's early work, both seem to me distinctly less successful fiction than the three satiric novels immediately preceding them. There are no impossible coincidences, no long orations on the worth of democracy and progress, not quite so many soaring abstractions. Yet both books are filled with the kind of romantic posturing characteristic of *Barren Ground* and *The Voice of the People*.

When Miss Glasgow abandoned comedy, I think she abandoned her true forte. Only in satire could she maintain the kind of objectivity about her people that made them believable and credible in their own right. Perhaps the impact of the Depression made the foibles of the upper reaches of society seem unimportant. Certainly light social comedy was no longer the favored literary form in book-publishing circles. Perhaps, too, the fact that Miss Glasgow was in poor health in the 1930s may have contributed to the reversion to more somber themes. At any rate, in *Vein of Iron* (1935) she returned for good to those who suffer and live without joy. She returned, too, to the plain folk, seeking to show, as the title of the novel indicates, the human will to endure.

Ada Fincastle, heroine of the novel, lives a blighted existence, as indeed does everyone else in *Vein of Iron*. Sexual passion becomes the stuff of tragedy again. Ada's boyfriend Ralph is accused of fathering the child of her rival, and he is forced—one is not sure in just what way—into marrying her. Then when a divorce is pending and he comes home, he goes out into the woods with Ada, and the result is another illegitimate child, this time for the heroine. Finally Ralph returns from the war and marries Ada, and they take up residence in Queensborough, but the going is never easy and Ralph is weak, misbehaving with a girl named Minna who lives next door. Ralph is injured badly in an automobile wreck, and then the Depression comes and they suffer grievously. Meanwhile, Ada's father, a philosopher, having long endured obscurity and want, finally dies, and at the end Ada and Ralph return to the Valley of Virginia, where they prepare to face the future together. " 'Never, not even when we were young,' she thought, with sudden glow of surprise, 'was it so perfect as this.' "

What is most striking about the novel is the passivity of the characters. None of them ever tries to accomplish anything; they sit back and take whatever is being handed out. As I have noted, it is never exactly clear just why Ralph accedes to the enforced marriage with Janet, Ada's rival, and the ruination of his promising law career. Nor is it really clear later on why Ada, having found herself in a family way, doesn't advise Ralph posthaste and thus ease her own anxieties. Still later, when Ralph proves so unreliable a spouse, one wonders why Ada doesn't inform him of her displeasure in no uncertain terms. Furthermore, if Ada's father is really so profound and noted a philosopher among all save his home folks, it is strange that he makes no attempt to secure a university position commensurate with his reputation. The inactivity all along the way seems lifeless, unreal; the characters do not behave like human beings. Like stone, they merely endure.

The net impact of *Vein of Iron* is not sympathy and admiration for Ada's rock-bound qualities, but something more akin to weariness. Ada never seems a thinking, hoping, acting person with whom the reader can feel any ultimate rapport. She remains masochistically locked within her own suffering, hewing to the dark side in spite of everything. The result is a bleak, depressing story, with no real passion in it save Ada's brief bacchanal in the woods. Ada does not merely learn to live without joy; she seems to prefer to do so almost from the start. The close of the novel, in which Ada and Ralph commence life in the Valley again and Ada declares that the best is yet to be, comes close to being incredible. All it can really signify, in the light of what has already transpired in the novel, is that being now properly burnt out and aged, Ada and Ralph can be sure that there will be nothing new coming along to give them much additional trouble—a debatable assumption at best.

Vein of Iron is notable for one thing. It contains one of the very few occasions in Miss Glasgow's work in which an act of sexual passion is portrayed as being in any way admirable or pleasurable for the participants. Even here, it is immediately followed by unpleasant consequences: Ralph goes off to war, and Ada conceives an illegitimate child. It is noteworthy that whenever Miss Glasgow treats sex seriously, from *The Descendant* through *In This Our Life*, it is made into something ugly and ruinous for all concerned.

Early in her career, Miss Glasgow wrote in *The Woman Within,* she took a manuscript of hers to a professional literary adviser, who promptly made improper advances: " 'If you kiss me I will let you go,' he said presently; but at last I struggled free without kissing. His mouth, beneath his grey moustache, was red and juicy, and it gave me forever afterwards a loathing for red and juicy lips."[59]

The tremendous physical revulsion and fear explicit in that description is surely paralleled in her fiction. Dorinda, for example, having in *Barren Ground* met only disaster in her liaison with Jason Greylock, spurns marriage in New York, and later when she marries Nathan Pedlar prefers an evening's work about the farm to the nuptial chamber. "I couldn't stand any love-making," she declares as condition to the union. Eva Birdsong's woes in *The Sheltered Life* come because her husband George is unfaithful, notably with a mulatto laundress. Annabel feels physical revulsion for the old Judge in *The Romantic Comedians*. When Abel Revercomb kisses Molly Merryweather in *The Miller of Old Church,* Molly is not enraptured: " 'Only I meant him to do it gently and soberly,' she thought, 'and he was so rough and fierce that he frightened me. I suppose most girls like that kind of thing, but I don't, and I shan't, if I live to be a hundred.' " Virginius Littlepage almost misbehaves with Mrs. Dalrymple in *They Stooped To Folly,* then returns home to find, almost as cause and effect, that his wife has died. Milly Burden of that novel, having succumbed to Martin Welding's charms, promptly conceives a child. As early as *Phases of an Inferior Planet,* marriage for the hero and heroine is quickly followed by desperate poverty and the death of their child, whereupon their union disintegrates.

Whenever sex is involved, it is sordid or it is disastrous, often both. One recalls Dorinda's curtain lines: "Oh, I've finished with all that. . . . I am thankful to have finished with all that." Only when the yearnings of the flesh are stilled can Miss Glasgow's people rest easy. Until that time, if indeed it ever comes, they are prisoners in the bonds of animal sensuality and can look for no true gratification of desire.

In her last novel, *In This Our Life* (1941), there is no true happiness or pleasure to be found for anyone. Written while its author was ill and often unable for months at a time to continue work, it is the story of impoverished townsfolk, vaguely members of the old aristocracy but for whom such identification has ceased to have any real meaning, and who suffer through various marriages and infidelities. The protagonist, Asa Timberlake, attempts without much success to comfort his wife, whom he loves only perfunctorily, and his daughters, whose husbands and intended husbands give them much trouble. During the novel Asa continues to discover what he knew at the outset, that life is indeed bitter. His daughter Roy learns that love is unattainable. His other daughter, Stanley, a predatory female, learns nothing at all. His wife's uncle William, a man of wealth, learns that he cannot take it with him. The cook's boy Parry, who wants a career in law, learns that Negroes who would elevate themselves usually have a difficult time of it. Once again all is passive, all is actionless; life happens to the dramatis personae, who learn a little more about the details of their plight, but do not change very much.

By comparison with a novel such as *The Sheltered Life, In This Our Life* is a tired, bloodless affair. There is no reason for Asa Timberlake's failures save his own essentially lifeless personality, and the novel takes its character from him. The struggle is over, lost; the classes are quite blurred and indistinct; the older people are worn out while the younger ones can discover no rhyme or reason for what they do or are. The Social History of Virginia has ended on a note of exhaustion.

Miss Glasgow planned a sequel to her last novel, to be entitled *Beyond Defeat*, but it was never completed. She died in 1945. Nine years afterward *The Woman Within* was released by her literary executors. To some, such as Marion Gauss Canby, the author of the autobiography "seemed to *me* in many ways a different person from the Ellen I knew."[60] To others, such as James Branch Cabell, the posthumous memoir seemed to confirm what they had long since sensed.

6. Miss Ellen

SHE HAS BEEN DEAD NOW for almost fifteen years. Her house on Main Street in Richmond, during her lifetime the last stronghold of social grace and charm in a neighborhood long since turned commercial, is now the headquarters of an educational center. Of her novels, two are still in print.

Her death, as Elizabeth Monroe noted, was not followed by any important critical revaluation.[61] Essays and chapters of books have been devoted to her work, but the only one that was primarily critical, rather than historical, was also primarily hostile. There have been doctoral dissertations, but these too have been mostly of an historical nature. She has been fitted into the Southern literary tradition, studied as a feminist, viewed as an examplar of certain American social and religious attitudes; but so far no full-scale esthetic evaluation of her novels for their own sake has been attempted. No literary critic of major stature has discussed her work.

Nor for that matter has there appeared in print a biographical study, though Marjorie Kinnan Rawlings was at work on one when she herself died. There are, to be sure, certain difficulties here that only time can solve, having to do with the matter of papers and of the feelings of still-living individuals. Her posthumous autobiography seems so to have angered some members of her family that they will not assist scholars seeking to gather material on her life.*

* I had myself some sharp evidence of this several years ago when, as associate editor of a newspaper in Richmond, I was approached by a graduate student at a North Carolina university who hoped to discover some contemporary reviews of Miss Glasgow's earlier work. In his behalf I ventured to approach several members of Miss Glasgow's family, to be informed emphatically that they did not wish "to cooperate" in any way with the endeavor! I have been told since that this hostility is primarily the result of *The Woman Within*.

The biography, however, will eventually come; we may be sure of that. If Miss Glasgow's reputation seems more and more based on her role as a figure in literary history, even almost entirely so, it is nonetheless quite secure—not so much for her role as chronicler of the social history of post-Civil War Virginia as for her place in the development of Southern literature in the twentieth century. Midway between the old romance and the latter-day realism she stands; in John Edward Hardy's words, "she is usually left, and probably will be for some time, rather gingerly straddling the near half century that was the period of her active career."[62] Her position would seem to be most aptly described by the word *transitional*. She occupies a position midway between those writers of the South's long Victorian twilight from whose esthetic she revolted, the Thomas Nelson Pages and James Lane Allens, and the post-World War I novelists of the Renascence, Wolfe, Warren, above all Faulkner—a writer whose work she thoroughly disliked.

She staked her ultimate reputation in American literary history on her attainments as social historian, chronicler in fiction of the inhabitants of the state of Virginia in transition from the Civil War to the New Deal. She would show a society in change, the old giving way to the new, the rise of the middle class, the decline of the planter aristocracy. But in the pursuit of this objective, as we have seen, Miss Glasgow had certain limitations, and her success at achieving such a social chronicle was seriously compromised by them.

Certain aspects of her social history seem quite valid both as fiction and as history (and as literature the two are indivisible; her social history is successful fiction, or it is not successful, save in an autobiographical way, either as history or fiction). In portraying the inadequacy of the aristocratic tradition when confronted with the demands of modernity, she achieved, in *Virginia* and *The Sheltered Life,* what was often memorable fiction. Likewise, *They Stooped To Folly* and *The Romantic Comedians* admirably capture the squirmings of a social class caught in a mold that no longer serves to define its members as human beings. In these four novels the social conflict, with all its problems of self-definition, is developed with insight and sympathy.

Other portions of the social canvas are much less convincing, much less solidly rooted in life. For she never understood *what* it was that was displacing the old. She never comprehended the nature of the new. First she sought to give it heroic virtues, but in so doing she failed entirely, for she was relying on the inapplicable standards of the old values. Then for a time, as in *Barren Ground* and *Vein of Iron,* she tried to assert the supremacy of the individual will over all human needs; but the only meaning she could find for such independence was a kind of death-in-life, an essentially escapist existence without comfort, compassion, or joy. Tired and ill, she moved at the last into the black, sodden pessimism of *In This Our Life,* in which all attempt at understanding was abandoned. She knew the old values were lost irretrievably; she could find no meaning for what had succeeded them.

In the final analysis, Miss Glasgow's level of achievement in her fiction rose or fell in accordance with the meaning she could give to experience, and this meaning depended squarely upon the meaning that she could find for her own personality. Insofar as she understood herself, so the Social History is understandable. Insofar as she did not, her fiction is likewise imbued with chaos and confusion.

In her four best novels, she wrote of her own class, and what its virtues and limitations were. This was part of herself, and she understood it very well indeed. But that part of herself she did not understand so clearly, she was not nearly so successful in portraying. By this I mean the independent woman, the modern who rejects the past as insufficient, the emancipated woman determined to rise above her class's social pattern into the life of reason and intellect, who will rely entirely upon the strength of her own will. These too she was, but the limitations of such attitudes she did *not* know. Indeed, she descried few if any limitations at all—and yet she wondered at her own unhappiness.

The Virginia in which she grew to womanhood was a changing world. I mean this not simply in an economic or a political sense—

the increasing inroads made by industrialism upon agriculture, the transition from government by an oligarchy of caste to a rural democracy. Rather, the dissolution brought about by the Civil War produced in Virginia, rather suddenly and belatedly, an eclectic, fragmented society, with few rules and codes. When Ellen Glasgow was born in 1873 (or was it 1874?), her class still possessed the one function that gave to it its life and its meaning, that of leadership. But already it was losing that function, and in the years of Miss Glasgow's life, leadership passed almost entirely from her class. An aristocracy without the function of leadership retreats quickly, as Mr. Trilling has noted, into snobbery—pride in status without pride in function. Those members of the Virginia aristocracy who continued to exercise leadership in public affairs did so not as aristocrats born to command but as new men. Senator Harry Flood Byrd, for example, bears an old and proud Virginia name, but his political hegemony owes little to it. There is nothing remotely akin to *noblesse oblige* about the Byrd Machine. What caste still exists in Virginia life is social, with only a vague correspondence to economics, and none at all to politics. It is thus essentially nonfunctional.

In Ellen Glasgow's lifetime, especially after the First World War, she could see the signs of social disintegration all around her. They are visible today as never before, in a thousand guises. The Olde-Virginia-Ham signs along U. S. Highway One; the sterile and artificial humbuggery of Colonial Williamsburg, Inc.; the machine politicians and lobbyists swarming about the statues of Washington and Lee in the State Capitol; the Room-for-Rent signs on the forlorn old mansions along Franklin and Grace streets in downtown Richmond; the plush suburban estates along the Cary Street Road on the West End, symbolizing as they do cultural-aristocracy-become-commercial-aristocracy—all these are the outward tokens of the social upheaval Miss Glasgow set out to chronicle.

As for the inward significance, we have Miss Glasgow's novels, both in their success and in their failures. For she never found a meaning for what had happened, save the negative meaning of loss. Possibly that *was* the only meaning to be found in it; but in that event, as Allen Tate said of Hart Crane, her task was then to explore and define the limits of her own personality and to seek to objectify the moral implications of the loss. But this is what too often she did not do; she stuck to her Social History, her attempt to discover and force a meaning into her experience. In this she frequently and largely failed, for she never satisfactorily explained, in the characterization and meanings she gave to her people, the true issues and meanings of her times.

She based her art on society, but all she knew of that society was what went on within herself. She was able by and large to see what *had been,* because that she could understand within herself. But she could never see what now *was,* because she could find no explanation for it within herself. All she could see was the fragments, and she could not fit them together.

The image that remains is not that of individual novels so much as that of a person, a woman, determined, courageous, who sought to impose upon her art and her times the order of her own personality. It was an unequal struggle, obstinate and foolhardy perhaps, and more than a little heroic, in the old way. The final impression is of the maiden lady in Richmond, regally holding court in her stone manse, determinedly discoursing upon Toynbee, Breasted, Santayana to famous visitors from afar. Beyond the windows the rooming houses and antique shops stretched out in all directions.

Notes

1. Edwin A. Alderman, "Introduction," in E. A. Alderman and Joel Chandler Harris ed., *Library of Southern Literature,* I (Atlanta, 1907 and 1909), p. xix.
2. *Ibid.,* pp. xix–xxi.

3. Charles W. Kent, "Preface," in *Library of Southern Literature*, I, pp. xv–xvi.
4. Rosewell Page, "Ellen Andersen *(sic)* Gholson Glasgow," in Alderman and Harris ed., *Library of Southern Literature*, IV (Atlanta, 1907 and 1909), p. 1847.
5. *Ibid.*, pp. 1848–49.
6. Rosewell Page, *Thomas Nelson Page, A Memoir of a Virginia Gentleman, by his brother* (New York, 1923), p. 197.
7. James Branch Cabell, *Let Me Lie* (New York, 1947), p. 241.
8. Ellen Glasgow, *A Certain Measure* (New York, 1943), p. 4.
9. *Ibid.*, p. 264.
10. C. Vann Woodward, *Origins of the New South* (Baton Rouge, 1951), p. 436.
11. *A Certain Measure*, p. 62.
12. *Ibid.*, p. 143.
13. *Ibid.*, p. 142.
14. *Ibid.*, p. 148.
15. Edwin Mims, *The Advancing South* (New York, 1926), pp. 215, 218.
16. Henry Seidel Canby, "Fiction Sums Up a Century," in Robert E. Spiller, Willard Thorp, Thomas Johnson, H. S. Canby ed., *Literary History of the United States*, II (New York, 1949), p. 1217.
17. Alfred Kazin, *On Native Grounds* (New York, 1942), p. 258.
18. Van Wyck Brooks, *The Confident Years, 1885–1915* (New York, 1952), p. 352.
19. *Let Me Lie*, p. 236.
20. *Ibid.*, p. 237.
21. James Branch Cabell, *As I Remember It* (New York, 1955), pp. 232–33.
22. Ellen Glasgow, *The Woman Within* (New York, 1954), p. 113.
23. *Ibid.*, p. 139.
24. *Ibid.*, p. 55.
25. John Edward Hardy, "Ellen Glasgow," in Louis D. Rubin, Jr., and Robert D. Jacobs ed., *Southern Renascence* (Baltimore, 1953), pp. 238–39.
26. *As I Remember It*, pp. 219–21.
27. H. Blair Rouse ed., *Letters of Ellen Glasgow* (New York, 1958), p. 134.
28. *The Advancing South*, p. 215.
29. *A Certain Measure*, pp. 59–60.
30. Maxwell Geismar, *Rebels and Ancestors* (New York, 1953), p. 235.
31. Lionel Trilling, "Manners, Morals, and the Novel," in Trilling, *The Liberal Imagination* (New York, 1953; Anchor Edition), pp. 203–204.
32. *Rebels and Ancestors*, p. 222.
33. *Ibid.*, p. 247.
34. *The Woman Within*, pp. 77–79.
35. *Ibid.*, pp. 100–101.
36. *The Woman Within*, p. 188; *A Certain Measure*, p. 82.

37. *A Certain Measure*, pp. 90–91.
38. *Rebels and Ancestors*, pp. 242–43.
39. *A Certain Measure*, p. 79.
40. *Ibid.*, p. 160.
41. *The Woman Within*, p. 243.
42. *Ibid.*, p. 271.
43. *Let Me Lie*, p. 231.
44. Louis D. Rubin, Jr., "James Branch Cabell Today," editorial page, *Baltimore Evening Sun*, July 6, 1956.
45. *A Certain Measure*, p. 154.
46. *The Woman Within*, p. 41.
47. *As I Remember It*, p. 232.
48. *The Woman Within*, p. 273.
49. *Let Me Lie*, pp. 235–36.
50. *The Woman Within*, pp. 243–44.
51. *As I Remember It*, p. 227.
52. Edward Wagenknecht, *Cavalcade of the American Novel* (New York, 1952), p. 275.
53. *A Certain Measure*, p. 243.
54. *Rebels and Ancestors*, pp. 273–74.
55. *A Certain Measure*, p. 201.
56. *Ibid.*, p. 204.
57. *Letters of Ellen Glasgow*, pp. 121–22.
58. *A Certain Measure*, p. 204.
59. *The Woman Within*, p. 97.
60. *Letters of Ellen Glasgow*, p. 372.
61. N. Elizabeth Monroe, "Ellen Glasgow: Ironist of Manners," in Harold C. Gardiner ed., *Fifty Years of the American Novel* (New York, 1952), p. 49.
62. John Edward Hardy, "Ellen Glasgow," in Rubin and Jacobs ed., *Southern Renascence*, p. 237.

PART II
A Southerner in Poictesme

1. The Bubble Reputation

AMONG TWENTIETH-CENTURY American novelists, James Branch Cabell is something of an exotic. Seemingly he fits in no solid literary "tradition," whether Southern or American or European. His days of renown were in the twenties, when the prevailing literary currents were naturalistic; yet no one in his right mind would think to attach that label to the fabler of Poictesme and Lichfield. From his Richmond friend and colleague Ellen Glasgow, he seems poles distant. Most certainly it would never have occurred to Mr. Cabell to champion the cause of blood and irony or to undertake any kind of social history. The term is worlds apart from the Cabellian universe.

He wrote most of his fiction about an imaginary, faraway land he called Poictesme, and the time he most often chose for his work was not the here-and-now but the hazy medieval. Furthermore, when on occasion he did consent to deal with modern Virginians, he was in no way concerned with the kind of material that any social historian would seize upon. Politics, class conflict, economic transition, the impact of modernity upon the Virginia aristocracy—what have these to do with Mr. Cabell's fiction, whether set in Lichfield or Poictesme? His people proceed with a total disregard for the burning issues of the day. "Veracity," he remarks in *Beyond Life,* "is the one unpardonable sin, not merely against art, but against human welfare." And again, "if 'realism' be a form of art, the morning newspaper is a permanent contribution to literature."[1]

Not only does his art sedulously avoid the contemporary scene with its contemporary problems; in those instances when moderns do inhabit Mr. Cabell's novels, they too are preoccupied with escape. Colonel Musgrave of *The Rivet in Grandfather's Neck* prefers genealogy to the public arena. The novelist John Charteris pridefully extols a literature on the Thomas Nelson Page model, telling Rudolph Musgrave that "I love to prattle of 'ole Marster' and 'ole Miss,' and throw in a sprinkling of 'mockin'-buds' and 'hants' and 'horg-killing time,' and of sweeping animadversions as to all 'free niggers'; and to narrate how 'de quality use ter cum'— you spell it c-u-m because that looks so convincingly like dialect— 'ter de gret hous.' Those are the main ingredients. . . ." Felix Kennaston in *The Cream of the Jest* finds soul-satisfaction only in dreams. In dreams, too, the Southern novelist of *The Nightmare Has Triplets* trilogy achieves his identity. In Mr. Cabell's last work of fiction, *The Devil's Own Dear Son,* the protagonist soon flees the tourist trade of St. Augustine for the customary Cabellian visit into the supernatural.

It is small wonder, then, that the term "escapist" has been applied to Mr. Cabell's work. Poictesme, the critics declared in the socially conscious decade of the thirties that followed Mr. Cabell's heyday, was a cloud-cuckoo land, having no purpose other than to divert and to amuse. His friend Ellen Glasgow, as we have seen, noted deprecatingly that his "delicate pursuit of the unholy grail wears, on high occasions, the semblance of allegory." Mr. Cabell's swift decline in both popular and critical esteem during the 1930s has on more than one occasion been ascribed directly to his failure to come to grips with the problems of his time. "Cabell and Hitler," declared Alfred Kazin in *On Native Grounds,* "did not inhabit the same universe."[2]

51

It is not surprising, too, that those who have written most about modern Southern literature tend to give Mr. Cabell's work only the most perfunctory attention. For, when dealing with a literature for the most part so directly and obviously Southern in theme and attitude as that of writers such as Miss Glasgow, Faulkner, Wolfe, Warren, Caldwell, and Welty, what seeker after regional significance is likely to pause for long over the strange allegories of Lichfield and Poictesme? Mr. Cabell was a Virginian, true, and of the First Families of Virginia at that, and in his heyday he enjoyed too large a reputation to permit discounting him entirely, but when so much that is more immediately Southern is available, the tendency has been to slight his work, and to dismiss his relationship to his native region as a simple one of escape. Because he found his own time and place distasteful, he fled into Poictesme.

In classifying Mr. Cabell as nothing more than a once diverting fabler and an esthetic expatriate, his critics have not acted without encouragement from Mr. Cabell himself. He glorified in his role as romancer, as we have seen, in his scorn of realism. And nothing seemed to irritate him more than for an interviewer to approach him as a Southern novelist. Faced with the prospect of an interview, for example, the dreaming Virginia novelist in *Smirt* vows anew that "I shall attempt to disguise, in resonant and shifty babblings, modeled after the general style of the New York *Times'* editorial page, my lack of firm interest in literary trends or in any of our younger Southern writers." Again and again Mr. Cabell expressed his entire absence of concern for the contemporary literary scene. He was uninterested in its writers; Joyce, Proust, Faulkner, Hemingway he did not read at all. The many Causes of his day he viewed with disinterest or disgust. In a revealing passage written and published during the Second World War, he told of his complete absorption with his writing, so that "the war, that inconceivable huge horror, becomes only a slight, disregarded annoyance now that writing drugs me. I have lived through too many years to expect human beings to behave rationally; and the war, as yet, stays endurably remote, in its more violent aspects, from tiny Poynton Lodge and my adjacent sedate seven acres in the Northern Neck of Virginia."[3]

At any rate, whether escapist or not, whether romancer or realist, whether Southern only by virtue of a retreat from the South, in the middle years of the twentieth century James Branch Cabell is a seldom-read, infrequently discussed writer. "I hear Oblivion tap upon the gate, / And acquiesce, not all disconsolate," he remarked in a sestina closing the revised edition of a book entitled *Chivalry*, in 1921, when his fame was at its peak, and subsequent events have borne out his prediction all too closely. As of 1958, but one of his several dozen novels is still in print, and that is *Jurgen*, in its day famed as a "dirty" book and, one suspects, available in inexpensive paperback edition today in part at least because of the lingering attraction of that notoriety. All of Mr. Cabell's other novels, all save the last of his almost equally numerous books of nonfiction, the autobiographical *As I Remember It*, are available only in libraries and in used-book stores. Many a study of twentieth-century fiction now ignores him completely.

All of which is in rather ironic contrast to his reputation during the heyday of his career, the 1920s. Then, H. L. Mencken led the band wagon for Mr. Cabell, and was joined by a goodly number of the most widely read critics in America. Vernon Louis Parrington, Sinclair Lewis, Burton Rascoe, Carl van Vechten, Carl van Doren, Joseph Hergesheimer—all united to sound his praise. Books about Mr. Cabell and his work were published. There was a symposium about him by a number of well-known writers. For several years he was perhaps the most talked-about author in America. Now, thirty years later, his novels are almost forgotten by most readers and critics.

To be sure, there are a few Cabell devotees who continue to pay him homage. One of the best chapters in Edward Wagenknecht's *Cavalcade of the American Novel*, for example, has to do with Mr. Cabell, whom Wagenknecht terms "a unique and incomparable figure in American fiction."[4] The Southern literature scholar Edd Winfield Parks has written several perceptive essays about Mr.

Cabell, remarking in one of them that the "part of his work which seems likely to endure will do so in spite of his manner, and because of his strong though perverse humanistic philosophy that guides and controls his best work."[5] And oddly enough, Edmund Wilson, who during the 1920s was severely critical of Mr. Cabell, has come to be one of his strongest and most unqualified champions. In a lengthy essay published several years ago in *The New Yorker*, Mr. Wilson deplored the fervor of the Cabell cult of the twenties, declaring that its effect "was eventually to leave the impression that its object was second-rate, and this is unjust to Mr. Cabell, whose distinction is real and of an uncommon kind."[6] So that Mr. Cabell does not lack for admirers in a few highly respected quarters.

In retrospect, the meteoric rise and fall of the Cabell cult is amusing, and among the persons most amused by it was James Branch Cabell himself. For not only had he foreseen his descent from popularity while the vogue was still at its height, but during the several decades when his name rapidly faded from the literary headlines, he kept right on writing his books and writing about his books, all the while casting a cold look at the whole business of reputation and recession. "When I reflect upon the half-century of pleasure which I have derived from mustering into print these cohorts," he declared not long before his death in 1958, "then the question does not in the least seem to matter, whether some few or none of these books will endure. I, here to become colloquial, I have had my fun, either way. That suffices me. And my conscience tells me, complacently enough, that I have made the most of my talents, such as they happened to be. For their limitations I disclaim being responsible."[7]

Whatever else may be made of him, there can be little doubt that in so saying he was absolutely sincere. For he never paid much heed to popular favor when he sat down to write his novels, any more than he devoted much concern to critical acclaim or the lack of it. He wrote primarily for himself, and all the evidence—fifty-two books of it—proves that he was his own taskmaster, and that nobody else was. "His one aim in life," H. L. Mencken wrote of him in 1928, "is to keep on writing books—books ever subtler, finer in surface, profounder, more savory, more penetrating, better."[8] Not once did he veer from that aim. The same sestina at the close of *Chivalry* in which he noted Oblivion tapping upon the gate ended with six highly revealing and never dishonored lines:

> For I have got such recompense
> Of that high-hearted excellence
> Which the contented craftsman knows,
> Alone, that to loved labor goes,
> And daily does the work he chose,
> And counts all else impertinence!

2. Poictesme-in-Virginia

"ELLEN GLASGOW AND I," Mr. Cabell has said, "are the contemporaneous products of as nearly the same environment as was ever accorded to any two writers. From out of our impressions as to exactly the same Richmond-in-Virginia, she has builded her Queensborough, and I my Lichfield; yet no towns have civic regulations more widely various."⁹

It would never occur to anyone to discuss Miss Glasgow's work without taking her Southern background strongly into consideration. Let us do what is much less customary, and look at James Branch Cabell in the same way.

As I have noted, Mr. Cabell's relationship as a writer to Virginia and to the South has customarily been ascribed, whenever anyone has seen any relationship at all, to a strong revulsion on his part to the contemporary Southern scene, leading directly into a fanciful flight into a cloud-cuckoo land. "Because he disliked the world he saw outside his Virginia home," Marshall Fishwick has written, "James Branch Cabell invented one inside his Virginia mind."¹⁰ An aristocrat to his fingertips, he looked out upon twentieth-century Richmond-in-Virginia, frowned upon what he saw, and conjured up a better never-never world of imaginary heroes, noble deeds, and grand passions, all of which were notably lacking in the modern-day South, and thus by inference he criticized the kind of life in which those qualities were absent. So goes the usual verdict.

Perhaps. Yet before accepting so simple and so pat a solution, it might be wise to examine a few of those "escapist" novels, and see just what kind of satisfyingly heroic life Mr. Cabell was purportedly setting up in contradistinction to the mundane present. Let us take a closer look at Poictesme and Lichfield, and at some of those Romantic Novels of Escape.

Figures of Earth (1921), considered by some to be Mr. Cabell's best novel, and certainly the seminal work in the multivolumed Biography of Manuel that probably constitutes Mr. Cabell's major achievement, has to do with a swineherd, Manuel, whose "gravest care in life appeared to be that figure which Manuel had made out of marsh clay from the pool of Haranton." Manuel soon postpones sculpting, however, and departs to seek adventure. He wins in turn the love of the queenly Alianora and the divine Freydis, but leaves both these more-than-mortal mistresses to win back from death one Niafer, an ordinarily attractive woman of no special charm, with whom he subsequently lives and rears children in the Duchy of Poictesme, the sovereignty of which he gains after considerable adventuring and maneuvering. His life at home with his middle-aged, not very exotic wife is not one of any special bliss or achievement, but even so he prefers it. Alianora might have given him perfect beauty, and Freydis's lunar magic could have enabled him to make his clay statuary come alive, but being a mortal, Manuel finds life with Niafer and the give-and-take of everyday companionship with his fellow mortals the condition that he can most comfortably endure. At the last he sees again the earthen figure by the pool at Haranton. "What is that thing?" he is asked. "It is the figure of a man," he replies, "which I have modeled and remodeled, and cannot get exactly to my liking. So it is necessary that I keep laboring at it, until the figure is to my liking and my desire." And with that the novel ends.

Now in just what way is Manuel's life an escape from the crass present? It would be hard to say. Manuel's heroic deeds have produced a dukedom, but what is it ultimately worth? He has not given life to the figure of earth he sought to sculp to his liking; there is still the third window of the palace, through which he cannot bear to look, and which represents all the things he had hoped to be, all the accomplishments he had meant to achieve and did not because he was mortal and had grown old without getting around to them. It can hardly be said that Manuel's life was especially satisfying to him. He had accomplished many things, but his primary goal—which he followed, it must be said, rather indifferently—remained largely unattained. The heroic possibilities of fanciful Poictesme have not produced anything more ultimately satisfying than might have been afforded had Manuel lived in mundane, unheroic Richmond-in-Virginia.

Escape into a more satisfying never-never land does not enter into the picture, then. For it is most clear that Manuel's life was *not* one of satisfyingly heroic accomplishment. He had his adventures, to be sure, was victorious in war, lucky in love. Yet the end result was that he was married to a matter-of-fact wife, with an ordinary family about him, and he could not bear to let his mind dwell on the vision of what he might have been. He had not creatively breathed life into the figure of earth, the statue of a man that he intended all along to complete and which was the idealized image of what he desired to become.

The cause of Manuel's failure was not lack of opportunity, not his crass and commercial times. Rather, it was his own inescapably mortal nature. He might have lived forever in the divine arms of Alianora. He might have let Freydis show him how to confer life on all his earthen figures. But being human, he preferred after all his own wife Niafer, the crippled girl with the sharp tongue, and in the process of winning her and wooing her he aged, and his opportunities slipped by him forever. He rode off with Grandfather Death, his life work unfinished. *Sic transit gloria mundi.*

So here is Manuel of Poictesme, who lived in an era when the heroic possibility was abundant, and yet he too found life not one whit more satisfying, at the last, or achievement any more meaningful for him, than might have been possible in Richmond-in-Virginia. What seems to be the moral is that all mortal works are essentially unsatisfactory. Manuel's only lasting achievement was his figures—and they were inadequate, because he was a mortal and thus inconstant to his art. The net effect is a denial of all possibility for mortal achievement in deeds, not because of crass times, but because of the nature of man. Only the figures, unsatisfactory, unfinished, remain after Manuel has gone. "We retain the *Iliad*," as

Mr. Cabell wrote on another occasion, "but oblivion has swallowed Homer so deep that many question if he ever existed at all."[11]

Even more interesting in this respect is *The Silver Stallion* (1926), which I myself consider James Branch Cabell's finest novel. Within its pages, which chronicle the growth of the legend of Manuel the Redeemer after his death, one looks in vain for heroic fulfillment. We follow each of Manuel's former companions as they attempt unsuccessfully to reconcile the growing deification of Manuel with the memory of the leader they once knew. Each meets his doom in his own way. Gonfal cleverly enjoys a queen's favors while her suitors go questing, and then is willingly executed. Miramon Lluagor, the artist, might have escaped the mundane life, but like Manuel he too foregoes the possibilities of escape into pure Art by fetching back his wife from the netherworld, and eventually he is killed by his own son, who wields the magic sword. (Mr. Cabell revelled in symbolism, Freudian and otherwise.)

Old Coth of the Rocks, who abhors the saintly legend of Manuel which is being created in Poictesme, goes off to find the real Manuel, but cannot recapture the past, and so dies in harness, beautifully, pathetically, remaining to the last the earthy, unregenerate old reprobate he always was. Guivric departs to seek the villain who is distorting and deifying the old saga, but finds it is himself; he bows, in other words, to the counterfeit legend and goes along with it. Kerin, too, thirsts for certainty and true knowledge, but finds out its meaninglessness and comes home to stay preoccupied with scholarly minutiae until he dies. Ninzian, the hypocrite, shrugs the whole matter off. Finally, Donander, the Christian God that Manuel believed in, winds up in a pagan heaven by mistake and passes his days by making his little creations of worlds, obeying the customary rituals.

At the last Coth's son Jurgen, the pawnbroker, talks with Dame Niafer, Manuel's widow, and decides that the growth of the legend may be all for the best. Everything has fitted into the legend, which is palpably false and humbug, and yet this has become more real than the truth. Who knows what is most efficacious? The legend of

Manuel in its very falseness has become a force for good. Jurgen does not know the answer to it all, but there it all is, nevertheless, and perhaps the legend is the best result that could be expected.

Certain aspects of *The Silver Stallion*, I think, seem most piquantly to serve as commentary on life in Richmond-in-Virginia during the youth of James Branch Cabell. He was born in 1879, just fourteen years after Lee's army surrendered. Not only his father but most of the adult males he knew had been Confederate soldiers. The Confederacy, its triumphs and defeats, it heroes, its loyalties and beliefs, dominated Richmond thought. Mr. Cabell has commented most amusingly and touchingly on this in numerous essays, one of the most noteworthy being the epistle to General Lee in *Let Me Lie*. The impact of the Confederate heritage on Richmond life was intense, and a child growing up amid the constant talk about the war could not fail to be strongly impressed by the atmosphere of battles and leaders.

If there was much discussion of heroism and glory in the air, however, it was past heroism and glory. The knights of the Confederacy who had, as everyone knew, fought so bravely and so valiantly in days gone by were now aging mortals, citizens of the city, and as the war years receded into the past, the myth of the war years grew. All Confederates became in their day of battle peerless and true; all engagements took place against overwhelming odds; flesh-and-blood soldiery who had fought profanely and unwashed in the hot, savage, summer campaigns now became in retrospect heroic, dauntless knights. During Mr. Cabell's childhood the legend was being industriously fabricated. Confederate Memorial Days, the numerous reunions of the army, the periodic dedications of statuary along Monument Avenue and elsewhere in Richmond, the storytelling of adults who had fought in the war and for whom, in Walter Hines Page's words, the war had constituted the most intense emotional experience of their lives,[12] all combined to raise a halo of myth about the graying veterans who frequented the parlors of Richmond homes and conducted the business and political life of the city.

But they were not mythological figures. They were men, with all the usual vices, habits, and compromises of men. As such, some of them did not hesitate to use the legend of the Lost Cause for political and financial profit, to talk of Duty while seeking emolument. Public and commercial life in Richmond during the 1880s and 1890s was not conducted upon a noticeably mythological plane, nor could it have been expected to be so conducted.

Yet it was the myth that was talked, if not acted. Cabell describes this phenomenon at length in the essay entitled "Almost Touching the Confederacy," in *Let Me Lie*. "They spoke," he says of his elders, "of womanhood, and of the brightness of hope's rainbow, and of the tomb, and of right upon the scaffold, and of the scroll of fame, and of stars, and of the verdict of posterity. But above all did they speak of a thin line of heroes who had warred for righteousness' sake in vain, and of four years' intrepid battling . . ." Their lately dead leader became "a god, or at any rate a demigod," and "there was no flaw in it when, upon tall iron-gray Traveller, he had ridden among them, like King Arthur returned from out of Avalon, attended by the resplendent Lancelots and Tristrams and Gareths and Galahads, who, once upon a time, had been the other Confederate generals." To a child, seeing these former Confederates walking about in everyday life, "it was confusing, the way in which your elders talked about things which no great while before you were born had happened in Richmond. . . . Richmond was not at all like Camelot or Caerlon upon Usk; and so you found it kind of curious that the way in which your elders talked, upon platforms, reminded you of your *Stories of the Days of King Arthur,* by Charles Henry Hanson, with illustrations by Gustave Doré."[13]

In private, Mr. Cabell pointed out, these same Arthurian adults used to talk of their legendary chieftains in somewhat different tones. Then they discussed such matters as famed generals who had upon momentous occasions been too drunk to sit properly upon their horses.

Your elders spoke also as to the final words of a more authentic hero, which, it appeared, were not the soldierly utterance that is set down in every Confederate Arthuriad, but a request for the bedpan; as to with how large thrift yet another pre-eminent idol of the Confederacy had behaved in renting out his renown, for advertising purposes, to a pack of gamblers, year after year; as to the manner in which an out-at-elbows paladin had apostatized in order to become an ambassador; and as to the quaint fury with which a half-dozen or more ex-chieftains of the Lost Cause were now publishing a surplus of inconvenient candors in their depreciations of one another.[14]

What the inhabitants of Richmond-in-Virginia were engaged in doing, Mr. Cabell declared, was nothing more nor less than constructing a mythology of the Old South for themselves. "They perverted no facts consciously; but they did omit, from their public utterances or from their printed idyllic narratives, with the tact of a correctly reared person, any such facts as appeared undesirable—without, of course, ever disclaiming these facts."[15] They built for themselves and the South a heroic ideal of stainless warriors and lovely ladies, an ideal quite beyond the reach of human beings anywhere. "To a child, who could not understand that for the health of human ideals every national myth needs to be edited and fostered with an unfailing purpose, the discrepancy was puzzling . . ."[16]

This process of mythmaking, set forth so quaintly by Mr. Cabell in *Let Me Lie,* is precisely the subject matter of *The Silver Stallion,* as any reader of that novel will recognize. The deceased Manuel's wife, Niafer, and her spiritual adviser, Holmendis, were with the aid of the population of Poictesme busily creating a national saint out of a most mortal and unsaintly man. The image of Manuel that finally prevailed was in few respects similar to Manuel. Those of Manuel's boon companions who had known the real Duke of Poictesme had perforce to come to terms with the myth, and in various ways they did so. In the end the myth, the legend of the godlike father of the land of Poictesme, triumphed. When Jurgen the pawnbroker ascends the lofty statue of Manuel that his widow had caused to be raised, he finds that the priceless jewels that adorned it were "one and all, and had been from the first, bright bits of variously covered glass." Jurgen had gone there at the behest of Niafer, who wanted to secure a loan with the jewels as security, for she, who had herself built the statue, had so forgotten what the reality was as to come to believe, too, that the glass was jewellery! When Jurgen ponders the matter, however, as we have already noted, he begins to realize that the statue of Duke Manuel was no mere fraud. Made though the statue was of counterfeit jewellery, and gross perversion and whitewashing of the truth though the legend of Manuel was, nevertheless

you knew the shining thing to have been, also, the begetter of so much charity, and of forbearance, and of bravery, and of self-denial—and of its devotees' so strange, so troublingly incomprehensible, contentment. . . . It was an ennobling and a picturesque reflection, that humanity had once risen to such heights; that mere mortal men had, through their faith in and their contact with the great Redeemer, become purged of all faults and carnal weaknesses, and had lived stainlessly, and had even performed their salutary miracles whenever such a course seemed requisite.

As Jurgen saw it, clearly the effect of the Manuel legend upon the succeeding generations of Poictesme had been beneficent. It was false, and yet it had civilized, ennobled, made virtuous those who believed in it.

Furthermore, there was the question in his mind, too, of which was the real Manuel—the flesh-and-blood one who was dead, or the imaginary Manuel of the myth? For Jurgen had played a key part in the creation of the myth of Manuel the Redeemer. As a child he had invented an episode in which, shortly after Manuel's death, he had seen the Duke of Poictesme raised from the dead and transported aloft. It was upon this evidence that the whole legend had subsequently been erected, and Jurgen knew it to be a false foundation. Yet thinking back on it, he wondered. For his fabrication had turned out to be "a most helpful and inspiring prediction which kept up people's spirits in this truly curious world; and cheerfulness was a clear gain. . . . There might, besides, very well have been something to build upon. Modesty, indeed, here raised the point if Jurgen—at that tender age and some while before the full ripening of his powers—could have invented out of the whole cloth anything quite so splendid and far-reaching? And that question he modestly left unanswered."

The myth thus conquers reality; reality becomes part of the myth; and there is no way whatsoever finally to distinguish between the two. Nor, for that matter, is it at all certain that to do so would be desirable.

Between the myth of the Redeemer of Poictesme and that of the stainless heroes of the South's Lost Cause there seems little difference. Mr. Cabell had created the one; he had during his childhood observed the other in the process of being created. In neither instance did the final product seem to bear more than a nominal relationship to the truth.

Of what importance is the myth, Mr. Cabell asks, whether for Poictesme or for Richmond-in-Virginia? He answers his question by declaring that mythmaking is the single most important fact of all human activity. He includes in his analysis not only the Confederate legend, or Manuel the Redeemer, but all mortal beliefs, including religion itself. Member as he was of Emmanuel Episcopal Church, Mr. Cabell believed strongly in the reality of religion—not because of any historical authenticity it might or might not possess, not even because it "explained" the mysteries of the cosmos. Manifestly, Mr. Cabell felt, it did neither. Rather he believed in it because the religious attitude itself, as the chiefest product of mythmaking, was Real. The only thing that remains in Poictesme after the mortal body of Manuel the Redeemer is dead and become dust and the tangible achievements of his reign are outdated and forgotten is the myth. That alone, therefore, is Real, because it alone continues to exist in time. "Men have, out of so many thousand years of speculation," Mr. Cabell has written, "contrived no surer creed than . . . that 'in matters of faith it is necessary to believe blindly.' Men have discovered no firmer hope than that, in defiance of all logic and of all human experience, something very pleasant may still be impending, in—need I say?—bright lands which are in nothing familiar."[17] Human ideas, as he remarks in *Straws and Prayerbooks*, "are of positive merit in that they make fine playthings for the less obtuse of mankind."[18] Life is indeed a dream, and to the extent that we partake of the dream, so do we live.

So to return to Richmond-in-Virginia and *The Silver Stallion,* it seems to me that far from that novel's being a form of cloud-cuckoo escape from the contemporary scene, it is a very perceptive inquiry into the nature of reality, and of a particular place's version of reality at that. Mr. Cabell looks at the world of men on Virginian earth that exists about him, and in their catch-as-catch-can attempt at a compromise between contemporary life and the demands of myth, he sees an inescapably human attempt to discover, through the making of legends, something real and believable in life. The mundane existence, business as usual, getting and spending, delving and spanning, are themselves insufficient to divert the participants. As Mr. Cabell remarks, "in the bared teeth of outraged reason, no one of us rests quite content to be a mere transmitter of semen, and to serve as one of many millions of instruments in life's inexplicable labor, used for a little while as such, and then put by, worn out and finished with forever. We appeal against oblivion."[19]

As for himself, well, even as a child he had begun to perceive the mythmaking activity for what it was, noticing the discrepancy between the Age of Heroes depicted in all good Confederate legendry and the inhabitants of the mortal and gaslit city of Richmond about him, and when he grew to manhood be began creating literature based upon such mythmaking. It was for him the only important activity. He could discover nothing else sufficiently real and deserving of attention. The one conviction he held about the everyday activities of humans, in Richmond and elsewhere, had to do with the briefness and evanescence of men and of what they did most of the time. To be alive was to be doomed in time: "We live *in articulo mortis;* our doings here, when unaffectedly regarded, are but the restlessness of a prolonged demise; and the birth-cry of every infant announces the beginning of the death-agony . . ."[20] Only mythmaking survived; of those things made by men, myths alone controverted time. "For we will to continue here, in the world known to us, to continue only as syllables."[21]

In creating and articulating myth, therefore, he was far from being an escapist from reality; rather, it was on precisely such terms that reality presented itself to him. Reality was scarcely to be found in everyday life; the myth of Manuel the Redeemer, as we have seen, was far more real than the events of Manuel's brief career. So-called realism in art, therefore, was, as Mr. Cabell expressed it, merely the art of paying attention to the mileposts along the way instead of to the journey itself.[22] The true realist was the romantic, the avowed mythmaker. The artists in the Cabell novels are all called wizards, sorcerers; and the wizardry constitutes the very reality of life itself:

To spin romances is to bring about, in every sense, man's recreation, since man alone of animals can, actually, acquire a trait by assuming, in defiance of reason, that he already expresses it. To spin romances is, indeed, man's proper and peculiar function in a world wherein he only of created beings can make no profitable use of the truth about himself. For man alone of animals plays the ape to his dreams.[23]

Thus James Branch Cabell's commentary on the worth of contemporary life in Richmond-in-Virginia and on earth in general. The legend was what solely and really mattered. So that one can indeed say that Mr. Cabell fled Richmond for Poictesme; but the implication that in so doing he sought to escape reality is hardly valid. He did not make of Poictesme a more satisfying world than the contemporary scene. Rather, Poictesme became for him the stage upon which all that mattered most about men became the direct and unsheltered subject of scrutiny, where what Mr. Cabell considered to be the customary mortal diversions and escape mechanisms were not operative, and where cosmological issues could be unashamedly faced. The meditations to which the statue of Manuel the Redeemer inspired Jurgen, for example, are hardly of less seriousness because they were occasioned by events in legendary Poictesme rather than by a contemplation of the statue of George Washington in Capitol Park in Richmond. Mr. Cabell's commentary is abetted, not hindered, by the fictitious locale. Believing as Mr. Cabell did in the supreme ephemerality of time and place, the particular connotations of the statue in Richmond could only have limited the application of his findings.

Of two customary fictional methods, he chose that of allegory, which involves dealing with the transparent in order that the particular application may be deduced therefrom, instead of symbolism, in which the locale is very much the particular and the universality is discovered in the details. It is not a very popular artistic method nowadays, perhaps because its straightforward approach can so easily become a device for banal moralizing. But in Mr. Cabell's hands there is nothing shallow or trite about allegory. It is developed in such complexity, and by so curious and so probing a mind, it is so well safeguarded against mockery by the constant use of a withering and undeceived comic irony, that any danger of sentimentality and moralizing is averted. The very appropriateness of Mr. Cabell's fable saves it from becoming vapid; the reader is too conscious of its application to shrug it off or to be merely diverted by it.

What the various Cabellian heroes do and think is often absurd; but in the absurdity there is peculiar sense, for even while we are amused we recognize only too well that what is being done or thought by the characters of the novels is no more ridiculous than what in our everyday life passes for intelligent conduct. At the end of every Cabell novel might well be affixed the words, *De te, fabula.*

3. The Human Comedy

I DO NOT INTEND by this to convey the impression that by and large the Cabell novels are pretty grim stuff. They are anything but grim. For Mr. Cabell is essentially a comic writer, and those who have placed him in the lineage of Boccaccio, Rabelais, Petronius Arbiter, Laurence Sterne are generally correct. Mr. Cabell is amused by the world; his novels are constructed upon that amusement. They are full of comic scenes.

One of the best of the Cabell novels, for example, is *The Cream of the Jest* (1917), which is built around one Felix Bulmer Kennaston, a novelist. Kennaston has somehow got hold of the Sigil of Scoteia, a kind of medallion which, if he will clutch it as he goes to bed, can transport him into a dream world of timeless adventure, in which he becomes the master storyteller Horvendile. Married though Felix Kennaston is to one Kathleen, he is in love with Ettarre, an immortal maid who represents all eternal, unattainable beauty, the beauty that creates and inspires romance and art, and which is never grasped because always pursued. At night, in dreams, Kennaston roams through history, explores time and space in company with Ettarre, and during his waking hours writes a novel which, much like Mr. Cabell's *Jurgen* of several years later, is misunderstood and vulgarized into a best-seller.

Finally Felix Kennaston finds the other portion of the Sigil of Scoteia, in his wife Kathleen's boudoir. She was Ettarre all along, he realizes, and neither could tell the other, for neither was aware of the other's role. Overjoyed, Kennaston leaves his half of the Sigil alongside his wife's half, and dreams no more. His wife, however, puzzled by the significance that Kennaston attaches to the Sigil, suggests that he discuss it with his friend Richard Fentor Harrowby, a student of the occult. Harrowby, she suggests, may be able to interpret the strange hieroglyphics on the Sigil.

But the wife's suggestion, as we learn through Harrowby, was not prompted by any belief in the occult. It is simply that the Sigil of Scoteia is nothing more than the lid of a cosmetics jar, manufactured by a company of which Harrowby is an owner! Harrowby does not so inform Kennaston, of course, for he does not wish to shatter his illusions.

The scene in which Harrowby "deciphers" the mystery of the Sigil is comic to the point of being absurd. All of Kennaston's fanciful theorizing is built upon something as unsubstantial as the seal from a cold-cream jar! The notion of the deadly serious Kennaston puzzling vainly over the secret message imprinted by the cosmetics manufacturer, finding in the tin disc the inspiration for wild and sublimely soaring flights into unreality, is almost wickedly ironic. Kennaston is in the direct line of such famous literary buffoons as Uncle Toby, Don Quixote, and the Socrates of *The Frogs.*

Yet, as with all great comic artists, there is pathos behind the buffoonery of Mr. Cabell. At the last, is Felix Kennaston actually the absurd, impractical, ludicrous dreamer that Harrowby and his other Lichfield neighbors think him? Has he really wasted his days, as even his wife Kathleen believes? Or has he instead achieved, in his dreams, what any man hopes only faintly to achieve—beauty, immortality, art?

We wonder, and for good reason. After all, Kennaston's pursuit of the radiant, unattainable Ettarre produces, in his waking hours, some very Cabellian novels, and therefore brings him impressively closer to those goals than his quite down-to-earth, realistic neighbors will ever come. Does it matter ultimately that the Sigil of Scoteia was only the disc from a cosmetics jar? For Kennaston it was far more than that, and by what standard of reality are we to say finally that he was deluding himself? If upon his valuation of the Sigil he built so imposing a superstructure of dreams, defied time and space, attained the quest of impossible loveliness, then which interpretation of the Sigil is real—his own, or the mundane world's? Eventually all that will remain of Kennaston will be the novels that grew out of the dreaming, and which in their imperfect way manage to retain a little of the wondrous vision of the dreams. But is this not far more than his neighbors will leave behind?

Built though those novels of Kennaston's may be upon an original absurdity, nevertheless they will continue to live when Kennaston, his wife Kathleen, Harrowby, and all the society of Lichfield—the so-called realities of the everyday world—have utterly vanished. Who was at the last the realist, Kennaston the dreamer, or Harrowby the man of practicality? *De te, fabula,* indeed!

So that Mr. Cabell's high sense of comedy, which dominates his work, is hardly mere frivolity and nonsense. It stems, rather, from a slyly ironic and sophisticated appreciation for the incongruities and the absurdities of human existence.

The famous *Jurgen* is likewise a comic book, including some episodes of rather low comedy. Tired of his wife, the nagging Dame Lisa, Jurgen the pawnbroker is granted the Faustian privilege of journeying through time and space, beyond the customary boundaries of life. He would regain his youth, and this means above all his aptitude for romantic love. So in succession he visits and tarries for awhile with Guinevere, who is all chivalrous and highborn beauty; Anatais, the incarnation of pagan, carnal delight; the Hemadryad Chloris, innocence, rustic bliss incomparable; and Florimel the vampire, all that a *femme fatale* can ever be. There is, furthermore, the chance for Jurgen to make love to Helen herself, who is also his childhood sweetheart Dorothy la Désirée, perfect, imagined, personally desired loveliness, the dream of one's youth, the embodiment of idealized, romantic passion.

In cavorting with these various maidens and matrons, Jurgen proves a "monstrous clever fellow," and Mr. Cabell's sense of pornographic symbolism is hard at work. Those who accused *Jurgen* of containing symbolism that is quite graphic were hardly mistaken. As was wryly pointed out by Mr. Cabell and others, however, one had to understand such things in order to recognize them in the novel. They are there, and Mr. Cabell, for all his protestations of innocence, knew they were, because he put them there. Which, however, is not to say that Mr. Cabell was composing pornography when he wrote *Jurgen*. It is rather that being essentially a realist (a term he abhorred), Mr. Cabell had his ladies and gentlemen act like human beings, and since sex is a fairly important human activity, Mr. Cabell's people gave some thought to it from time to time. The true test for pornography is whether the sex exists to further the characterization, or whether the characters are in the novel to permit the sexual references. In *Jurgen*, as in Mr. Cabell's other work, the amatory activity is simply a vital part of the characterization and never the final object.

Jurgen is a novel about marriage, its pros and cons, its compromises, its essential but often exasperating importance to society. As a young man, Jurgen loved one Dorothy la Désirée, but was rejected by that damsel in favor of one Heitman Michael, a bearish lout. Later Jurgen married Dame Lisa, a descendant of Manuel the Redeemer, who proved a shrew. At the outset of the novel Jurgen longs for his lost youth, when he was a poet, and when he and Dorothy la Désirée were sweetly in love with each other. Enabled to ride aboard a centaur toward the setting sun and past it, Jurgen goes back in time to the days when Dorothy was fond of him. But Dorothy will have none of this middle-aged man who calls himself Jurgen; it is a young and romantic Jurgen that she favors. Later Jurgen sees Dorothy as she is in his own time, and marvels that so corpulent, unglamorous and flagrantly promiscuous a woman could have been the maiden who had once set his youthful heart palpitating and his senses afire.

Next Jurgen is enabled to wander into the domains of mythology, wearing the shirt of Nessus which protects him in his travels. With various damsels he experiences all the varied delights of conjugation. When finally, however, Kochschei, creator of time and space, gives him his choice, he prefers to have Dame Lisa reinstated. He is used to her; he is not young and world-conquering, but middle-aged and accustomed to his conveniences and routines, and life with Dame Lisa is what he has learned to expect. As has been remarked, *Jurgen* is something of a plea for monogamy, but a quite unromantic, disillusioned plea, based on the thesis that one's wife, who does not understand one, is part of the human compromise with ideals, and essential to man's condition. Man might indeed attain immortality, the stars, the heights of romance and art, but being man, he prefers marriage.

Here again, the legendary trappings of Poictesme and the coming and going of supernatural beings do not produce an escapist romance; instead, they only heighten the irony, for all such romantic settings prove of no avail against the invincible and incorrigible humanity of the characters. The purpose is emphatically not romantic, but realistic—Mr. Cabell is decidedly engaged in pointing out what humans are, not what they should be. H. L. Mencken rightly declares him "really the most acidulous of all the antiromantics." The "gaudy heroes" of the Cabell novels, he notes, "in the last analysis, chase dragons precisely as stockbrokers play golf. . . . Art, argues Cabell, is an escape from life: a doctrine quite beyond challenge. The artist seeks surcease from reality by creating an ideal world. *Soit!* But once he has moved into it he finds to his dismay that it is made of the same silicon, carbon, aluminum, oxygen, hydrogen and calcium that make the real one."[24] The shirt of Nessus, then, the centaur, and Kochschei only serve to emphasize Jurgen's human condition. What he finds beyond time and space is still more mortality.

The considerable success of *Jurgen* led reviewers of Mr. Cabell's subsequent novels to compare each with that book, and as Mr. Cabell notes, the findings were monotonously similar. Either the reviewer discovered that the new book was *Jurgen* all over again, and thus inferior to it, or else the reviewer found that the new book was not like *Jurgen*, and therefore inferior to it. Such is ever the way of book reviewers, of course, and Mr. Cabell professed not to value the findings of book reviewers very highly; who were the reviewers, after all, to patronize hard-working novelists by consenting to praise their work or to judge them by finding their books faulty? Book reviewing, Mr. Cabell averred, was at best a rather pointless and presumptuous business.

Yet it must be admitted that there is truth to the charge that Mr. Cabell tended to repeat his themes. He appeared to regard his plot situations as mere frameworks and to use them automatically and habitually while concentrating on the variations he could work on them. Such a device as a visit to the world beyond this one, where time and place did not apply, became for Mr. Cabell much like a kind of sonnet form, to be repeated regularly in each novel while all the originality was expanded on the particular encounters in such a world.

His art is built upon certain recurring themes and devices. The reader of his novels soon comes to expect them. Yet the effect is not one of monotony; one always looks forward to seeing what Mr. Cabell is going to do with those themes and devices this time. First and foremost, of course, is the magic journey into the supernatural, which always ends not in escape and contentment, but in the decision to return home to mortal compromises and the known limitations of existence. Each time the visit to heaven or hell only results in a discovery that such places are not essentially different from anyplace else. Their inhabitants, whether Kochschei or the devil, angels or minions of Satan, all turn out to be bored, weary creatures, and their doings provide the visitor from earth with no more lasting satisfaction, no more unendurable torment, than life on earth. Such journeys, and the results of them, tend always to reinforce Mr. Cabell's oft-repeated conviction that since we are mortal men, life on earth is all we can ever imagine, and our struggles to escape that limitation are no more than romantic dreams.

A counterpart to this is another Cabellian motif, the quest for unattainable, superhuman beauty. Time and time again Cabellian heroes yearn for a loveliness that is not subject to the usual human limitations, and sometimes they find such loveliness, but they always discover that it too is unsatisfactory. Gerald Musgrave, in *Something About Eve,* continually searches after beautiful women who will not cloy, as his mortal mistress cloys, but each new daughter of Eve turns out to be but a replica of Evelyn Townsend. Jurgen, visiting eternity, turns away from fair Helen's bed, because he knows that only by so doing will he be able to preserve the illusion that she at least is more than mortal. Florian de Puysange, not so wise, seeks out the lovely Melior of his dreams in *The High Place,* and she soon proves to be no different from earthly mistresses. Mr. Cabell's golden lads and lasses all come to dust, for such is ever the way of golden lads and lasses.

But if the quest for unattainable beauty never succeeds, it is nonetheless a continual quest. A reiterated Cabellian theme is that of the young man who falls in love at an early age, loses out to another suitor, and spends much of the rest of his life pursuing the image of his youthful love. Logically he knows that the lady in question has, like himself, grown middle-aged, and the dream of her eternally youthful loveliness is of no human creature but of love itself. No more pathetic moment exists in a Cabell novel than that in which the older man confronts the woman who was once the vision of perfect delight for him and realizes that she is simply an old woman now, in no way ethereal or forever fair.

The Cabell hero is a prisoner in time. That is the only ultimate fact about man as Mr. Cabell saw him. Everything man does is a vain attempt to extricate himself from chronology. The central truth about man is that he is mortal and must die, and as a mortal he cannot know fulfillment. For the artist, as a man, life represents a continual diminution of his urge to create, a hopeless and failing quest for the impossible act of pure creativity.

Yet of all man's activities, only art can offer any hope of survival; works, worldly honor, glory, all are forgotten when the man who attains them is forgotten. Only art endures beyond death, and, as has been noted, that most uncertainly and erratically.

But though individual lives count for nothing, and even art survives tenuously and without logic or consideration of merit, one conviction nevertheless runs through Mr. Cabell's art: that the nature of man is indomitable. Man knows neither why nor how he exists, but he *is*. Without in any way idealizing man—no one, indeed, saw his limitations any more clearly—Mr. Cabell presented him as a creature of courage and endurance, the central image of all creation. For Man dreams; his whole life is dependent upon dreams, many of which he cannot for one moment prove or demonstrate, but which even so afford him his only and supreme hope. Like Marcel Proust, Mr. Cabell was convinced that we are tending toward something that we do not know, but which is better than we are, and that this expectation and conviction are both inescapable and crucial to all that we think or do. He declared:

I prefer to take it that we are components of an unfinished world and that we are but seething atoms which ferment toward its making, if merely because man as he now exists can hardly be the finished product of any Creator whom one could very heartily revere. We are being made into something quite unpredictable, I imagine; and we are sustained, through the purging and the smelting, by an instinctive knowledge that we are being made into something better. For this we know, quite incommunicably, and yet as surely as we know that we will to have it thus.[25]

So that at bottom, all of Mr. Cabell's cynicism, and his fond and fastidious mockery of human pretense and conceit, is based upon a kind of visceral and rock-bound humanism, a conviction that in the very absurdity of his dreams and his playing, Man is demonstrating that he can and will survive. For Mr. Cabell, the mythmaker is supreme, because it is he who by dreaming confutes the very nature of mortality. "And it is this will that stirs in us to have the creatures of earth and the affairs of earth, not as they are, but 'as they ought to be,' which we call romance. But when we note how visibly it sways all life we perceive that we are talking about God."[26] Further than that, Man cannot know, though he will keep trying to find out; but that conviction is of itself a sign that Man is not here for nothing.

What, then, of Mr. Cabell's much-vaunted romanticism, his castigation of realism in literature as being essentially trivial? It all depends on what is meant by "realism," and as Edmund Wilson says, when Mr. Cabell denounced "realism" he was being a trifle supercilious and "apparently unaware that to glorify the 'dream' as against the 'real' is merely to express a preference for one kind of fictional convention rather than another."[27] Certainly what most critics mean by "realism" applies to the Cabell novels. And that is, an essential concern with the here-and-now, an attempt to show what life is. To use, for example, James D. Hart's definition in his *Oxford Companion to American Literature,* realism is the "term applied to literary composition that aims at an interpretation of the actualities of any aspect of life, free from subjective prejudice, idealism, or romantic color. It is opposed to the concern with the unusual, which forms the basis of romance. . . ." If that definition is admitted, and it is probably as good as any, then it is difficult to see wherein Mr. Cabell's novels are anything but realistic. His fabled land of Poictesme, his flights into a magic world devoid of the limitations of time and space, are in no way essentially "unusual"—for once in never-never land, Mr. Cabell's heroes immediately discover that existence there is conducted under exactly the same conditions as in "real life." Men are still men, women are still women, diversions are still diversions, human limitation is still a necessary human condition; the apparent escape serves primarily to emphasize just those facts.

Mr. Cabell's concern is always with what life is, what men really are. His heroes' chief discovery is always the inescapability of their mortal roles. To Mr. Cabell, that fact is reality, life. His object is to delineate exactly what being human means. Sometimes, despite his abhorrence of the word, he gives himself away by admitting overtly that realism is a just criterion.

So, to the defense of Cabell the realist, as accused by Cabell the alleged scorner of realism, we call in as witness James Branch Cabell himself. In the preface to *The Cords of Vanity* we find him discoursing, in the third person, on his youthful attitude toward that book and to its protagonist, Robert Etheridge Townsend. Of himself as a young writer he declares that:

In the main point of every creative writer's business he did, I think, succeed. He created, that is, a character which has some actual vitality. Townsend has appeared to me, during my revisions of this book, rather real. I find, to be sure, that my present-day opinion of Townsend as a person is not quite the self-evident opinion of the young man who first wrote about Townsend. I think, for example, that Townsend does change during the book's progress. And I detect in Townsend somewhat less of depravity and more of foolishness than his youthful creator, I suspect, ever intended to exist. But the point is that I can agree with him, and, for that matter, with all the most unfriendly critics of Townsend, in considering Townsend as one considers an actual human being. The point is that, to my so much older and perhaps age-damaged eyes, Townsend seems rather real. There the defense rests. . . .[28]

There the defense rests indeed.

4. A Shelf of Books

BACK ONCE AGAIN, AND FINALLY, to Richmond-in-Virginia. We have remarked the peculiar applicability of James Branch Cabell's alleged escapism to everyday life in that city as he saw it, and we have remarked, too, the distinct differences between his Lichfield and Ellen Glasgow's Queensborough. They are far-reaching differences indeed, for they reflect a vastly disparate attitude toward life and art on the part of these two Richmonders, who grew up in the same city and wrote their novels at about the same time. Here is Miss Glasgow, highly serious, appalled by fate. Even her three comedies of manners seem very much in earnest when compared with Mr. Cabell's work. She takes her people's plights very seriously; at bottom, it is no joking matter. And on the other hand, here is Mr. Cabell, mocking, sardonic, quite amused at the petty distresses and concerns of his fellow men. It will all come out in the wash, he seems to say; a thousand years hence and it will make no difference to anyone.

Yet the two of them were equally dedicated craftsmen. Both thought the writing of their books the most important thing in the world, and both were all too well aware of the pitiless nature of the gaze that posterity casts upon all art and artists. If Miss Glasgow seemed somewhat more concerned with advancing her present-day reputation than Mr. Cabell did, if she guided reviewers, lined up critics, and bent all her energies to insuring a favorable press in her own time and for as long afterwards as possible, still, that is understandable and excusable in someone whose force of character and intellect had led her to defy the mold into which refined Richmond gentlewomen of her time and place were supposed to fit. She forsook bravely the customary comforts of female existence in upper-class Richmond society; small wonder, then, that she tended to be overly anxious to prove to others that her choice had been justified. And as for Mr. Cabell, if he in his turn wore the mask of ennui, sophistication, smugness even, just a bit too obviously and self-consciously, that too is not altogether inexcusable in one whose whole tradition and rearing had taught Leadership, Position, Participation, and who rather daringly turned his back on Serious Matters in order to face up to art. Both Mr. Cabell and Miss Glasgow made their daily adjustments, to be sure. But both of them knew that what mattered most for them, what mattered at all, was their books.

They were different kinds of people; they lived quite different lives. Well, no matter; both of them risked all for their craft; both, to use Mr. Cabell's words, daily did the work they chose, and counted all else—or almost all else—as impertinence.

The result of their endeavor is a long shelf of books—fifty-two for Mr. Cabell, twenty-three for Miss Glasgow. Now both of them are dead, and Richmond-in-Virginia goes on its way.

It goes on its way indeed. Mr. Cabell and Miss Glasgow changed nothing; what they saw in their native city, one can still see, by and large. Mr. Cabell's devastating dissections in fiction and nonfiction alike, Miss Glasgow's earnest appeals for blood and irony, have not perceptibly altered the conduct of life in the former capital of the Confederacy. Richmond is Queensborough, it is Lichfield and Poictesme still.

With this exception: that there exists the shelf of books. And so there is a dimension to the life of Richmond-in-Virginia that may very well outlast its corporate dimensions, that may preserve its identity far beyond the lifetime of the present inhabitants—far beyond, even, any changes or adjustments, moral, material, spiritual, that might sometime in the future come to pass. For the image that James Branch Cabell and Ellen Glasgow have created will last, and any quarrel that "real life" might have with it is unimportant, inconsequential. During the remainder of its recognizable days Richmond-in-Virginia must labor under the yoke of being more importantly and more memorably Lichfield or Queensborough than its own self—a handicap, to be sure, that, as Mr. Cabell especially would have noted, would trouble it not at all. Yet for better or for worse, there it is: life in Richmond-in-Virginia, man on Virginia earth, 1900–1950, set down that all may see, and, more than that, transformed into the clearer image of literature. It is a kind of permanence, an identity beyond time, the hope even of an immortality, treasured in a shelfload of books. One might conclude by quoting again from the *Chivalry:*

> For I remember; this is she
> That reigns in one man's memory
> Immune to age and fret.

Notes

1. James Branch Cabell, *Beyond Life* (New York, 1927; Storisende ed., Volume I), pp. 31, 200.
2. Alfred Kazin, *On Native Grounds* (New York, 1942), p. 231.
3. James Branch Cabell, *Let Me Lie* (New York, 1947), p. 5.
4. Edward Wagenknecht, *Cavalcade of the American Novel* (New York, 1952), p. 353.
5. Edd Winfield Parks, "James Branch Cabell," in Louis D. Rubin, Jr., and Robert D. Jacobs eds., *Southern Renascence* (Baltimore, 1953), p. 261.
6. Edmund Wilson, "The James Branch Cabell Case Reopened," *The New Yorker,* April 21, 1956, p. 29.
7. James Branch Cabell, *As I Remember It* (New York, 1955), p. 240.
8. H. L. Mencken, *James Branch Cabell* (New York, 1928), p. 10.
9. *Let Me Lie,* pp. 247–48.
10. Marshall W. Fishwick, "Cabell and Glasgow: Tradition in Search of Meaning," *Shenandoah,* VII, 3, Summer 1957, p. 24. See also Mr. Fishwick's essay, "Two Roads From Eden," in *Modern Age,* II, 4, Fall 1958, pp. 404–407.
11. *Beyond Life,* p. 262.
12. Burton J. Hendrick, *The Life and Letters of Walter Hines Page* (New York, 3 vols., 1922–1925), I, pp. 90–91.
13. *Let Me Lie,* pp. 145–46.
14. *Ibid.,* pp. 154–56.

15. *Ibid.*, p. 154.

16. *Ibid.*, p. 156.

17. James Branch Cabell, *Straws and Prayerbooks* (New York, 1924), p. 42.

18. *Ibid.*, p. 167.

19. *Ibid.*, p. 278.

20. *Ibid.*

21. *Ibid.*, p. 183.

22. *Beyond Life*, p. 21.

23. *Ibid.*, p. 38.

24. *James Branch Cabell*, pp. 22–23.

25. *Beyond Life*, p. 270.

26. *Ibid.*

27. "The James Branch Cabell Case Reopened," *loc. cit.*, p. 141.

28. James Branch Cabell, Preface to *The Cords of Vanity* (New York, 1929; Storisende ed., Volume XII), pp. xvii–xviii.